Cł

Changing Hearts

Making good decisions about relationships and separating

JILL BURRETT

ALLEN & UNWIN

By the same author

To and Fro Children
A guide to successful parenting after divorce

First published in 1993
Allen & Unwin Pty Ltd
9 Atchison Street, St Leonards, NSW 2065 Australia

National Library of Australia
Cataloguing-in-Publication entry:

Burrett, Jill F.
Changing hearts: making good decisions about relationships and separating.

Bibliography.
Includes index.
ISBN 1 86373 314 0.

1. Separation (Psychology). 2. Interpersonal relations. 3. Adjustment (Psychology). 4. Divorce. 5. Interpersonal relations—Decision making. I. Title.

306.89

Set in 10/11.5pt Times by Graphicraft Typesetters Ltd, Hong Kong
Printed by Kim Hup Lee Printing Co Pte Limited, Singapore

10 9 8 7 6 5 4 3 2 1

Contents

Preface

I'm frequently struck by how many people have real difficulty doing things about their relationships: to commit, separate, compromise, make changes, have another try, recover, or make do. They get stuck, feeling dissatisfied and uncertain, and don't know how to move onwards.

This book is going to help you:

1 Make better decisions for yourself through being better informed about your options and their consequences.
2 Acquire greater awareness of yourself and how you affect others in key relationships.
3 Feel a greater sense of personal mastery and effectiveness as a result, so you increase your chances of coming out in front after making important changes in your partnerships.

Almost everyone faces a major relationship challenge at least once in a lifetime, but most of us don't handle ourselves all that well in an emotional crisis. Amidst phenomenally sophisticated technical advances in so many areas of everyday life, we're lagging way behind with developing knowledge and skills for our emotional and interpersonal lives!

Most people don't plan their love-lives very wisely, often becoming involved or leaving in a rush of emotional reactivity, unable to apply the astute analysis that they can readily put to use in other areas of their lives!

Perish the thought that the excitement and spontaneity of love be lost to the cause of serious deliberation and forward planning! But by understanding yourself and what you do in love will certainly help you to make better choices, help you realise the importance of attending to relationships actively, and help you manage the disappointments and the necessary adjustments more effectively.

Most of us would like to understand ourselves and our impact on others better so that we can feel more aware and in command of our lives. Increasingly people want to explore interpersonal relations so as to take charge of their emotional life, their workplace, and their social and love partnerships more effectively. There's a new curiosity borne of a desire for increased self-knowledge and individual responsibility, and a questioning of traditional reliance on professional experts to help us when the going gets tough.

If you're deciding whether to separate, you'll want to be sure it's really the right move for you. You certainly owe it to your partner, your children and your future partner(s) as well as to yourself to do all you can to manage your decision effectively, with all the consequences of your change of heart faced head on. If you're having to face up to being left, then you'll find that a better understanding will help your adjustment considerably.

Facing a key relationship issue usually brings disconcerting pressure to answer questions like: are my doubts about my marriage normal or serious? How can I recapture that magic I had which I can only find now by having affairs? Can relationships really change or am I stuck with this? What will happen to my relationship with my children if I give them a stepfather/mother? How can I be sure I make a better go of this relationship? How can I show him/her that we really can be happy together? I'm not happy, but is that enough reason to leave? How do I know whether my unhappiness is in my marriage or something else? Should we stay together for the sake of the children?

The list of relationship dilemmas goes on and on, but we often come back to the basic question: how will I know what to do? If only some expert could tell us, we say to ourselves when we feel stuck, almost as if a reliable forecast was available, a formula we could apply to work out the answer, to save us more indecision, heartache and doubt.

Only *you* can find the answer, by becoming more informed and insightful about yourself, about human nature in relationships and separations, and about all the practical and emotional consequences of a change of heart. Only by taking active steps like this, rather than just reacting and marking time, will you be able to move on from feeling stuck to heading in the right direction.

I can remember going through months of soul-searching from when I first had serious doubts about my marriage to when I actually made up my mind to do something about it, and still more months before the situation was actually resolved. At first I suppressed all my feelings of disquiet and was quite unable to allow the idea of questioning the quality (and hence the future) of my marriage to enter my ordinary thinking. Then there was guilt, obligations, breaking a commitment, causing pain and hurt, personal disillusionment, a sense of not really knowing who I was and what I wanted out of a relationship (or even out of life); the frustration of trying to discuss my feelings (and I knew I must) when I wasn't even really sure what they were myself and knew they would hurt him, etc. etc.

That's all years ago, and today I find myself (by a series of opportunities and obligations rather than through strategic forward planning!) advising, counselling and writing about relationships, separations and parenting in blended families. So I know that deciding what to do about your love-life and getting on with it is something that many people, including those who seem successful and 'together' find incredibly hard and often don't manage very well. I wanted them to have a special kind of informative and practical book to read. A book about how love relationships change, about deciding what to do about it, about changing love into something more like what you want, and about how to separate in the best kind of way if that is what you decide to do.

I am very grateful to Patrick, and others at Allen & Unwin who read the plot, for latching onto the idea of this book with such gusto. I hope that their response is a sign that it's a topical subject for as many people as I believe it ought to be! Special thanks go to the many people whose personal dilemmas broadened my experience and knowledge, and provoked my thoughts about decision-making and management both in and out of love; to Geraldine Hunt for putting her insight, literary talent and good humour into various drafts, ensuring I kept on the straight and narrow and didn't get too long-winded; and to my husband for his enthusiasm for the project throughout.

JB, 1992

Introduction

Most of us who separate find that disappointment, anger, guilt and hurt drive us in a reactive, sometimes impulsive way along the uneven route from disenchantment through to separation and eventual resolution. We tend to seek the support and guidance of family, friends, or new partners to help us along emotionally. Or we go it alone without any human reference points, perhaps relying on professionals to tell us how to arrange our affairs for the future. We see the changeover in our attachments as a major disturbance to our usual equilibrium. This feeling of disruption is our emotionality interfering with our usual vision and problem-solving skills. We are unable to rely on our usual rationality because so many confused and unmanageable emotions get in the way.

Mismanaging breakups

Of course it's in the very nature of love that when it frustrates us, we either want to escape or to hang on, we think trying to work on the problems together is sure to be too difficult or pointless, or we desperately try to make our partner stay. Usually we can't prepare with our partner for parting, and one of us runs out on the uncomfortable emotions of it all, never really having time to pause and discover what really happened, and leaving confusion, misunderstandings and uncertainties around us for quite some time. The scene is then set for a period of continued misunderstanding between you and your partner because it feels impossible to negotiate disengaging jointly from the relationship you built together.

We all want to make good decisions, the best for everyone involved, and plan the future with wisdom and forethought if we can. We don't want to find out later that we'd have been better off handling decisions differently, or wishing we'd made different ones. For the sake of our personal effectiveness and sense of self-worth, we all need to be able to look back into the past, and say that on the whole we don't wish we'd done things differently, that we've made a good adjustment to it all.

Falling in love and making a commitment are major events, but certainly the first time around we don't usually put enough thought into what's really happening because we're busy enjoying and being guided (even blinded) by the intensity of our feelings. Thank goodness for the delights of romantic love, but beware the many challenges!

Later on the process of facing up to major changes in love, whether it's to leave or to try and improve a relationship, usually makes you ask important questions about yourself, often for the first time. It makes you search for insights about couples; about what makes your partner tick, and what you *really* think and feel about things. You feel a pressing desire to know more about what makes people behave the way they do; what happens to people in marriages; how to find more insight and awareness so you'll know what to do and be more in touch with likely consequences. Self-reflection, talking to friends, getting into counselling, reading, thinking, trying things out and having reviews with yourself and your partner are all valuable ways of acquiring more insight, awareness and sensitivity so that you can make good decisions and become enriched by your disappointments as well as by your triumphs.

The story of Michael and Sue

Here's an example of the way a troubled relationship can get stuck. It shows some of the many questions a couple must often face on the way towards a resolution.

> It took us almost two and a half years to eventually arrive at a kind of separation. During this period I didn't ever want us to part. Throughout I believed that I loved my wife (and still do, although my feelings about her have changed in significant ways). In all our

lengthy discussions which were often very emotional I came to realise how limited our relationship of thirteen years had been in many ways, something I hadn't really considered before. Many things about how it had developed were my fault though I didn't realise it at the time. Sue has always maintained that she continually tried over the years to get me to see what wasn't satisfying her, with no result. We discussed this one point at length, and she began to see that perhaps she hadn't ever communicated them well enough. Why this should have been so, if she was really that unhappy, was a puzzle. We both came to understand better how family life, travel, job preoccupation and other things operate to prevent you attending to what's happening—or in our case not happening—at the time. It's not just a matter of being too busy. It's also that in a way you become dependent on all those things which help you avoid other things that are hard, like really negotiating changes before patterns of coping with your relationship get set in, and time just goes by. For Sue perhaps being a mother to our three children gave her emotional satisfaction of a kind she wasn't getting from me, enabling her to manage her frustrations about me, at least for some years.

She has always maintained, since we started talking about separating, that she cannot really communicate with me, that I don't really understand her. This has frustrated me enormously (it still does), because when I'd ask her to define what she meant by real understanding between partners (so that perhaps I could do something myself towards achieving it), she couldn't ever tell me. She'd say you just feel and know when it's there.

We had counselling together over quite a long period, but I always had the idea that her starting point for trying to do things to enrich our relationship was different to mine in important ways. I was hopeful and ready to embark on whatever program of relationship-building exercises we could find for however long it took for us to both see some hope. I believed we could make it. But somehow this never got off the ground, leaving me feeling she had never really believed it was possible from the start. She'd implore me to do something to show her I could learn to give her what she wanted, but I still don't really know what this something was!

A very significant shadow was in the background for both of us during our efforts to resolve our problems. This was a relationship she had started while we were away from home which was still active though at a distance. She said it had enabled her to discover and feel many of the things she thought were lacking between us. It amazes me that we were able to discuss this relationship in a reasonably civilised way, because I really think if it hadn't been for him we might never have separated, and the possibility of him becoming part of our family with her in the future enraged me. I was having enough trouble coming to terms with our family breaking up and losing touch with our children, without this.

Michael has been in the difficult position of remaining committed to his wife and family, while having to gradually face up to the inevitability of an eventual separation. He's had to learn to accept his wife's position, even though he will probably never be able to understand it. And he'll always have a niggling feeling that she could have made a decision to make it work, despite her doubts. Sue's version of the events is no less troubled, even though she was the one with the greater dissatisfactions:

I went through periods of real depression while we were trying to negotiate about our family. I wasn't functioning well. I felt relief when Michael was away on business, because when he was around I began to be short-tempered with the children. But I couldn't decide what to do with my life. I know I only felt tempted into another relationship because of what was wrong with my marriage. After years of smouldering frustration I knew I was vulnerable to the temptation of attention from another man, and I was consumed with guilt because doing this goes absolutely against my moral values. I couldn't tell whether what I'd found with John was something that could progress into a really satisfying relationship with time. I've never hated Michael and I will always value many of his qualities. I often think leaving him would do him a favour in the long run, because he'd then be able to find something better too.

For a very long time I've felt really stuck, burdened down with chronic uncertainty about what I should do. I think if it hadn't been for our three children and my worries about the impact of our separating on them I would have left to explore things with John. And I think if it hadn't been for the possibilities of this relationship I would have stayed with Michael. There wouldn't have been any point in leaving to be on my own. I've tried to work out whether I just want too much from a relationship, expecting the relationship itself to make me happy, instead of trying to find happiness on my own. I'm very confused about all this, because I know that all I really want in life is a satisfying relationship. Is it so misguided to want that? When Michael used to say to me, 'Tell me what it is you don't get from me', I couldn't really tell him what it was our relationship didn't have.

Michael was always saying 'We can improve things if only we both really try', but he never did anything to make me feel there was really any hope. I've been desperately frustrated trying to tell him how I feel, and he just doesn't understand. At times I've felt really frightened at how angry I am about everything.

He's very worried about the future with the children (so am I), and is convinced he's not going to be able to have a meaningful relationship with them. It's terrible when he gets all emotional about this. The last thing I want is to destroy his sense of fatherhood. I'm much more certain than he is that the children won't lose touch with him, and I'll always be encouraging their contact, especially if John and I get together.

It's taken much longer than I thought it would to resolve things, and I still feel depressed and really stuck. But we have at last told the children that we're probably going to separate, and agreed that Michael will move out soon, which is a big step, although in many ways this hasn't made me feel any better about things. We didn't want to tell the children until we were reasonably certain, or we'd be putting them through unnecessary worry for nothing. We put off doing this for ages because we knew we should do it jointly, and I was afraid of how the children would react towards me if Michael insisted on being honest with them and telling them it was me who wanted to leave the marriage and not him.

I still don't really know which way to go and feel that putting up with the kind of relationship I can have with Michael may still be an option for me.

Sue is experiencing to the full the real anguish of deciding what to do about what she thinks is wrong with her life. She is only partly aware of her dependency on relationships and how they operate for her. This couple's story illustrates the ongoing nature of getting separated, the 'stuckness' that is often felt in the process, and the many factors like parenting responsibilities, alternative relationships, and different expectations which have great bearing on how you handle relationship dilemmas. Although for Sue and Michael the process has been slow and distressing (and it often is), they have done one thing which will help make their futures better than if either of them had fled from the relationship sooner. They have worked on the issues together, so they gain some understanding of their own and each other's point of view, and kept their concern for each other and their children a priority, and know that they have really tried. This is hard to do.

You too may be in the throes of facing up to your marriage breaking down, but don't feel able to do anything about it yet; you may be embarking on, or well into a second or subsequent major relationship and starting to wonder more about what you do in partnerships so you don't repeat your disappointments; you may be struggling with your relationship with your 'ex' which you really must nurture because of the children; you may be trying to adjust to an imminent or actual separation which you didn't want and believe needn't have happened. Whatever your starting point for wanting to think further about relationships, the aim is a successful resolution of your own particular set of dilemmas.

Relationships are seldom static. They have phases and stages which are influenced by events like parenting milestones, financial circumstances, health factors and occupational changes etc. Making changes in relationships, and in particular getting separated, is also a process which goes through stages. The process generally takes its course in its own time, although how you contribute and react along the way will (or won't!) help it along.

What to aim for

Successfully resolving your relationship uncertainties involves many tasks. These are some you should be aiming for.

1 To know what you want out of a partnership. This means understanding how the things you want reflect needs you have which work for you as well as against you; the extent to which you can reasonably expect to find these from a partnership; what demands your particular needs place on a partner; the ways in which these needs operate to make you hang on to relationships which may not be workable ones, or want to leave relationships which could be improved.

2 To know how you could be operating differently in your relationship. You could be relying on your relationship to provide you with happiness, self-esteem, security, and a reason for living. Your relationship could be overloaded if you aren't doing enough yourself to find these things.
3 To know how your needs for separateness and connectedness in a relationship vary by the day, the week or the month; how these normal variations work in you and how they affect your partner. This is 'interpersonal vision' and it's essential to satisfying relationships.
4 To know how to communicate effectively in a relationship. You need to be able to express your needs and feelings without threatening or confusing your partner; and to allow your partner to do this with you.
5 To know when doubts about your relationship mean you need to make some changes if you're to stay in it; knowing whether changes are possible, how long to go on trying, how to make changes that will stick, how you'll know when you've tried everything.
6 To take responsibility yourself for your changing needs and feelings so that you can approach what may need to be a major change in a relationship, including getting out of it, with courage, foresight and emotional honesty.
7 Knowing what all the effects of finishing are going to be on everyone as well as yourself. There are two aspects to this. First, taking into account your partner's position as you see it, as well as how *they* say *they* feel it! And how they'll respond to your change of heart. It's unlikely they feel the same way as you do about the partnership, and longstanding communication difficulties will have put you both out of touch with each other's real feelings. Second, there's the children. You need to know all about the myths and the certainties about separating and children, to help you weigh up your decision before you make it.
8 Understanding how being left when you weren't prepared for it affects you and your emotions, self-esteem and interpersonal relations. Knowing how to muster the resources to recover sooner rather than later from this upheaval by cultivating positive attitudes for getting on with life.
9 To be able to really see how a new relationship affects how

you feel about your ailing one. It often limits what options you think you have, distorting your vision of the future. To be realistic about how the life you think you'll have after separating will really affect you.

10 To make the switch to being cooperative co-parents after being disenchanted lovers, whether it was you or your partner who was the prime mover towards the decision to separate.

11 Being able to look back on the period of change and adjustment and say to yourself that there's nothing you could have done differently which would have helped anyone any more. It all still makes sense, you've been enriched by the experience and have no important regrets. Having prepared yourself for it all, there was nothing that cropped up that you didn't anticipate.

12 Knowing enough about yourself and your relationship to be sure that there's no alternative to splitting up. Enough that is, to prevent you ending up further down the track discovering that in lots of ways you wish you hadn't gone through with it all and were still together. This comes from acquiring an increased sense of your own mastery of your emotional self, enabling you to make informed and responsible decisions in your life and in your relationships.

This long list is what coming out ahead with relationships is all about, and every item on it is important. To move towards achieving them you need to know more about behaviour in relationships than most people usually do, so that you can apply this to yourself and get more insight into how you function. You can't make good decisions about intimate partnerships until you have some idea of how your own emotional reactivity clouds your thinking and how you respond to your partner. You need to inform yourself of the facts and probabilities associated with all the options you have, before you choose one.

How this book starts to take you there

In many ways the objectives in this book amount to a philosophy of personal potential and self-responsibility. To achieve them you need to have decided you want to do something about your life.

This is going to involve active planning and doing which, especially when it comes to your key relationships, is only possible through systematic fact-gathering and self-review. Achieving the goals you set for yourself in life, extending yourself to the point where you are exploring your own personal potential a lot of the time, growing and changing with every experience you have, is an exciting route to be on, even if you did start out on it because of a disappointing marriage or long-term relationship!

The pages that follow will take you on a comprehensive journey, beginning at the basics about human needs and behaviour in relationships and in love, how maleness and femaleness contribute, how successful relationships are created and maintained. The first four chapters are a preparation for thinking about separating from a position that is more informed and insightful, to help with systematically weighing up all your options.

Chapter 5 is all about the consequences of separating for children and for parenting. You'll need to think hard about this to help you decide whether to separate, as well as to apply what you've learnt to your parenting from separation onwards.

Chapter 6 examines the question of alternative relationships and how they affect separation decisions, because they are often what first prompts you to reappraise your existing one.

Chapter 7 is about moving towards separating, the turning point in your relationship. You'll learn how it affects both partners, what your options are at this point and how to get closer to a decision. Chapter 8 discusses how to master the period immediately after a decision is made and out in the open. Trial separations, getting back together and making practical arrangements for being separated are some of the topics.

Chapter 9 anticipates some new issues that you'll be facing once you've separated. It helps you find out how close you've come to successfully changing partners, how to go on cultivating helpful attitudes for your own continued growth, your relationships with past, present and future partners and with your children.

Everything about relationships involves reciprocity, so the parts of this book that don't seem to apply directly to you still concern you because they probably apply to your partner. *Seeing things accurately from another's point of view and taking it into account is essential for successfully mastering relationships at every stage.*

You'll find the coverage gives you the beginnings of real insight to a level that equips you with more confidence to make the choices you face, without holding you back from the urgency of your immediate priorities. Delving into the complex recesses of the adult psyche and putting the knowledge gained into good everyday use is a fascinating process, but it's time-consuming. So throughout you'll find challenges to your thinking in the form of check lists and tasks, designed to promote decision-making and action for your immediate circumstances.

Perhaps your curiosity to go further once you have changed direction will have been stimulated, because you feel empowered as a result of tackling your relationship dilemma the positive way. Many very readable and extremely helpful texts are available which will take you further, and some suggestions are included to help you continue your journey of self-discovery.

1 Understanding selfhood and dependency

Tying the proverbial knot is probably the single most important decision you make in your life, affecting many people apart from just you and your mate, especially if you go on to have children. The consequences are far-reaching! And yet we're not very good at selecting life partners. We're attracted to people for all sorts of different reasons and our good judgement gets mixed up with the delights of falling in love. Many of these reasons don't make a good basis for a long-term partnership. What's more, we're often not aware of the way our own personal needs and feelings guide the way we behave with our partners, so that not only is our ability to select a suitable partner to begin with limited by how self-aware we are, but so is how we manage the ongoing relationship over time. Our needs quite unconsciously often override our real feelings and opinions about people, and what we want from them and for them.

We are all influenced by tremendous pressure to couple. Young adults, even though they may not see themselves as wanting to marry and have children too soon, need and seek intimate relationships once they've left behind the security and daily human contact provided by their family of origin. It's not so surprising since from birth (even from conception) we are dependent on people close to us for our survival and our gradual steps towards increasing independence. We are a gregarious species, and whether we're prepared to admit it or not, we can only really function in relation to others. A good part of why we get into relationships is to avoid loneliness and find reliable companionship.

Everywhere around us our culture emphasises the ideal of a satisfying, stimulating and even glamorous intimate partnership as essential to being a completely successful person. This creates a subtle kind of pressure to get on with the business of sharing and caring. It's expected of us and we expect to do it. Getting off to a flying start by falling in love is a very powerful force in making our decision to tie the knot. Our own needs for closeness with another and for regular sexual expression, combined with this pervasively commercial emphasis on idealised couples and families, and the urgency of falling in love, drive us forcefully into the pursuit of relationships, often before we've had enough life experience to really know who we are as separate beings, and what we really want out of life and partnerships.

With all this, it's hardly surprising then that many of us have quite a few false starts and disappointments along the way, or find ourselves stuck in relationships that don't seem to be going anywhere!

If you are someone who like so many of us has an imperfectly formed sense of self at the time you make a romantic commitment, then you are likely to have problems in relationships. As young adults, say in our early to mid-twenties when many of us marry, we are only just working out for ourselves, independently of the influence of our families, who we are and what we want out of life. It's the very beginning of our relationship career, and you probably look back on this time now and think how little you really knew about life then! *It's the combination of an unformed self and the mystery of the love experience that so often is a recipe for relationship difficulties.* We need to understand our dependencies better, and the importance of self-definition to managing our relationships effectively, not only so as to understand our pasts better, but so as to use this insight productively in the present. And for those others for whom being in a relationship is necessary in order to feel a sense of identity at all, this task is particularly important.

Many people in troubled marriages know, though usually in a confused kind of way, this feeling that their real self is not being expressed, and don't know how to express this without getting away from the relationship. We'll learn more about falling in love and how it can misguide us in the next chapter. Here we're going to examine the very subtle and frequently misunderstood notion of the self, which begins developing long before a person is exposed to the hazards of falling in love.

> Looking back on my first marriage I can see now what an incredibly blinkered view of life I had in my early twenties. I thought I was madly in love, and I used the intensity of the feelings, which were entirely based on a fantasy of this man—generated out of my own intense needs at the time—to tell me he was Mr Right. Love sure is blind, because I really turned this person into someone he never was. Before we got married, I had some quite serious doubts, but I ignored them because I assumed that everybody had doubts, it was normal! What would I do with myself if I didn't marry? Although at the time I don't think I saw myself as desperate, I so wanted to get 'hitched' that I suppressed my own warning signs! I thought I ought to be getting on with marrying, because so many of my friends were!
>
> What it was really about, I can now see, was me not wanting to face finishing university and taking on the real world by myself; wanting someone to look after me, a 'respectable' way of getting away from largely imagined ties of family and cultural pressures. Marriage provided a way of acquiring social status for myself the easy way (he had professional standing), and a response to the intoxicating sensation of someone older and worldlier than me apparently thinking I was marvellous. I mustn't have thought I was!

This story shows how many confused pressures often guide a person to make a commitment. This woman in her early twenties met her considerable dependency needs through over-investing in a relationship. It's a very common position, and doesn't necessarily always lead to a bad match. The important thing missing for this girl was that she didn't know how her own needs were working at the time, so she couldn't take them into account. They therefore blinded her to what was really going on in the relationship, and to factors which might have enabled her to assess its suitability with more vision. As things progressed she began to feel a growing sense of her undefined identity and found she could only come to discover her separate self outside of this relationship. She had gone headlong into the apparent security of a commitment, to avoid facing underlying uncertainty about herself and her future, giving herself a feeling of self-definition through marriage. Her very dependence on her husband was what made it seem impossible to resolve this within the marriage.

Knowing ourselves

Your self-image is the single most crucial factor influencing what you get out of life and what you are able to give to people and projects. How favourably you regard yourself determines with what confidence you approach life, what risks you are willing to take, how able you are to create opportunities for yourself to acquire and refine skills, how much you need people to make you feel whole, and hence how you manage relationships. If, for some of the many reasons we shall be considering, your self-image is vague or uncertain then it's likely to be rather negative, and you'll be someone who relies to an unhelpful extent on your relationships with other people to define your self-image for you. This is how self-image, or selfhood is linked to dependency.

All of us, especially those of us who are parents and teachers, know how important a sense of self is. We naturally want to praise and encourage our children's emerging skills and reinforce their attempts at mastery. We do this even when we know their attempts are misguided, and we try to play down their mistakes so as not to discourage their efforts. We are enacting our belief in the importance of feeling good about yourself.

If you feel good about yourself most of the time (you know and accept the bad bits and how they work against you, as well as how the good bits work for you) then you'll be able to communicate what you want from life and from people. You'll have the spiritual and emotional strength to approach life and relationships with people in worthwhile and satisfying ways.

Where does this crucial factor called selfhood come from, and what do we really mean when we sometimes feel a sense of nothingness about ourselves? How do we know when we have a positive strong self, or when we don't?

The development of the self begins at the beginning of our lives. As infants, we arrive in the world with all that it takes to develop a sense of our own unique set of strengths and limitations, our essential character. We have a raw energy for life which both delights our caretakers and strains their patience. The interaction of this energy with the kind of world we find ourselves in determines how our sense of self develops. If we cry loudly and often, we will discover our separateness from our caretakers (the beginnings of selfhood) by how well they meet our needs for whatever they decide they think we want when we cry. We learn how much tension is generated when they fail to soothe us effectively. We begin to learn our separateness from the world by making connections between movements of our limbs and bodies, the experience of willing these movements and the consequences. We learn the limitations of our power by finding we cannot control our circumstances much, although we go on wanting to. It is the kinds of opportunities we get to experiment with our worlds, incorporate the results of those experiments, and go on with more experiments, that provides the continuous, lifelong process by which we acquire a knowledge of who we are, our strengths and our weaknesses, and how we feel about them. Our caretakers must be able to allow us these opportunities for experimentation, at the same time giving us consistent love and praise for our efforts.

In other words, it is the way in which this life force or energy affects other people and the rest of the environment about us that determines how we develop from infancy onwards. We come into the world with certain temperamental and physical characteristics of our own which shape the way we express our energy for life. Our extreme dependency on our immediate caretakers (particularly our need for their approval), means that our opportunities for this expression, and how it is shaped by the responses it gets lies very much in our parents' hands. Their temperaments and values dramatically affect how we are permitted to give expression to these energies we are born with, and how governed by them and hence by other people we grow up to be. We will do and become whatever it is that seems to get our parents' love and approval. Every family setting is unique, and all of them have peculiarities of some kind. However much we might want to get the important task of parenting right, no one really can. There are skeletons of a more or less benign kind in every family closet, however much outward appearances may be happy and successful.

So it's the characteristics of our family that determine how in touch with ourselves we grow up to be, and how good we feel about ourselves. To illustrate this, consider a mother who finds herself married and into parenthood perhaps sooner than she might have preferred, and has a career-dedicated husband with little time for shared family responsibilities. She feels isolated by the ties of a small baby and anxious about the responsibility of motherhood. Her eagerly developing infant starts to crawl and explore, and her anxiety makes her restrain her child from the slightest possibility of risk, dirt, mess or injury. The slightest sniffle brings out the medicine collection, the slightest change in baby's habits is a major concern. Her own anxiety prevents baby from experimenting naturally, from taking any risks at all.

She controls and defines baby's entire experience, and her child begins a pattern of relying on her to define its reality. She gives over her entire self to the cause of her child's wellbeing, so doubtful is she of her own worth, which prior to marriage she sustained through dedicated work. Meanwhile her child is on the way to growing up dependent on another for validating and defining its entire experience. Mother has not given her child opportunities to explore and experiment with its own being. Mother's own uncertainty about herself means she needs to have this child develop a personality and attributes which will meet her own needs. There's plenty of love, but it's always conditional on the child's behaviour conforming and reassuring her. Father is not available to counterbalance Mum, and his lack of availability means the child so craves his affirmation that she feels unloved and becomes dependent on trying to be whatever might bring his attention. A dependent parent is producing a dependent child, who has little idea of her own needs and feelings, and her real self, which she will skilfully shield, is a frightening void of uncertainty.

In families where parents allow their children, in a secure, consistent and loving setting, to experiment with the world and with people, and to be different and separate from themselves and from their own hopes and needs, there will be room for the development of individual potential and balanced, loving relationships. In families where there is a problem of some kind in one or other parent which limits their availability to their child, the child will tend to blame themself for the lack of parental attention and even for the problem itself. Buried deep beneath a dependent personality are usually feelings of fear and self-hatred. A person who has been unable to develop a self-image cannot possibly feel good about their own nothingness.

Since we're gregarious by nature, then isn't dependency on people and on relationships a normal thing? Of course we're all influenced, sometimes profoundly, by other people's behaviour and feelings. *It's when we can't distinguish between our own feelings and behaviour and those of others that we depend on other people to define ourselves.* Our decisions are governed by what we think our dependents need and expect from us more often than by what we really want for ourselves. We allow ourselves to use concern and support for other people's needs to prevent us meeting our own. We cannot experience wholeness or function adequately unless we ensure we're being actively cared for and needed by another. We don't know that we are living our lives like this, it's a pattern we acquire from our families, and we skilfully conceal the extent of our dependency. Yes, we are all dependent to some extent, we all have periods when we need more support and direction from others, and other times when we feel really on top of things, secure about our own opinions, decisions and actions. It's understanding our own dependency and how it affects our choices and our relationships that's important.

Codependency

Some people then, because of a limiting family upbringing (short on love, big on control) are never able to find their real selves, and hence their real potential and unique creativity. They spend their lives hiding their denied selves behind a poorly-functioning relationship in which they strive to change (but in fact often nurture) their partner's perceived faults. These faults may be centred around a dependency on alcohol, another toxic substance, gambling, or an eating disorder, for example. Much has been written and put into practice in the last decade about the relatively new concept of codependency. This has stemmed from concern about the relatives of addicted people, and how they themselves may be contributing to the maintenance of the problem behaviour by needing the relationship with the addicted person. Its newness is in the way it's now being described, and the more hopeful pathways out of it that have thus been generated, rather than in the condition itself.

Codependency is not confined to people associated closely with addictive dependencies, however. All relationships are codependent to some extent, but healthy relationships are not codependent at the expense of either partner's own authentic selfhood and productivity. Unhelpful codependency is surprisingly widespread in ordinary-looking relationships.

Relationship addicts hide behind a cause—sustaining a partnership—to avoid looking at a terrifyingly frail, impoverished real self. Often loving and self-sacrificing on the face of it, their apparently worthy behaviour has underlying it a need to control others by seeking to change and cure them, so as to avoid looking at themselves. They depend on others for their self-esteem, skilfully denying their own frailty through dedication, good works and untiring devotion. They are addicted to people to make themselves feel loveable, but their underlying emptiness means they can never get enough to fill the void. Women, nurtured as they are to be nurturing, involved as they are with valuable roles as wives and parents, are often trapped without realising it in codependency; in time experiencing generalised dissatisfaction or chronic physical symptoms, fatigue or depression.

Every misuser of food, alcohol or prohibited drugs is codependent. They use a mood-altering substance to block out underlying conflicts from their childhood. They tend to attract a codependent partner who needs their 'symptom' to maintain a secure relationship for themselves. It is secure because the problem gives them a reliable cause to devote themselves to curing, and behind which to mask their own frailty. It operates something like this: if you are needed by another, it helps ensure they'll never leave you. Involving yourself in a relationship with someone codependent themselves, a workaholic, an alcohol abuser, a sexual philanderer, for example, ensures a secure relationship through which you gain your much-needed self-definition.

If you are codependent you will tend to feel responsible for people who are close to you. You'll feel afraid of making mistakes and you'll strive to present a competent image. You'll be worried that other people will leave you so you'll try not to make demands on them, and do things to please them even when you don't want to. You'll have difficulty expressing your opinions to people, and will feel trapped and chronically dissatisfied.

The fact that dependency is learned, we are not born with it, is good news, because it means we can make changes through insight and determination. The key to freeing yourself from unhelpful dependency is one which unlocks the denial which covers it, opening the door to real awareness of your circumstances so that changes can be made.

How dependency affects relationships

If you over-invest in a relationship, relying on it as a substitute for expressing your own separate energy and creativity, you will demand more from your partner than they can give. Your dependence will prevent you from giving your partner what they want to meet their real needs. In particular, their need to partner a whole rather than a part person. You need to be able to achieve your potential as an individual from within yourself, not just through others, or you'll find yourself vulnerable to the uncertainties of love because the partner in whose service you have been living may leave you because you seem lifeless. You may blame your relationship, unfairly, for not achieving things yourself. The inadequacies you see in your relationship may become the focus of all your dissatisfactions and lack of personal progress, because you cannot afford to examine your own contribution.

You may, with admirable worthiness, be looking after an elderly parent, a partner with an alcohol problem, or a handicapped child, to the point where you never have time to do anything for yourself. This limits your own development. It's not that parenting and caring for others isn't entirely worthwhile, it's when looking after others is such a dominant part of your life that your own need to do it may mean you aren't giving the right kind of care anyway. Whatever you do, your partner doesn't stop drinking or working compulsively, and nothing changes.

This story of a breakup shows how a dependent wife contributed to the eventual split. Happily she eventually became better able to see how she had contributed.

> I was quite devastated when my husband told me he wanted us to split up. I hadn't realised he was that unhappy and when he told me he'd fallen for someone else I felt all the usual things like I was being traded in, like small thanks for all the years of nurturing I'd put into family life, enabling him to put so much into his work and

career ambitions. The worst thing I think was feeling like I didn't get given a chance to try and improve things before he'd made his decision. And when I tried to get him to tell me what was wrong with the marriage he couldn't (or wouldn't) talk about it. Him shutting off from me and not ever giving me the chance to try and understand his point of view was almost the worst part of the adjusting I had to do. I felt completely abandoned.

Years later I could see that I'd been blind to what was really happening. At the time he broke the news I reacted in panic, protest and rage like a vulnerable child who'd lost their security blanket. I couldn't see how life could possibly go on without him. I begged and pleaded with him believing that I really loved him and that no one else in the future would do for me. I even thought that my declarations of love would be enough to bring him back. After all, a person's genuine committed love should be enough to conquer all, shouldn't it?

Eventually I came to realise that throughout our marriage I had depended on him for everything—my reason for living, a structure for my daily routine, a source of self-definition, and a person to rely on for important decisions. I wasn't operating as a separate person in my own right, and my dependence on him (which I mistook for love) was what drove him away eventually.

For the first years he probably needed me to need him that much, but later came to find it too demanding. I guess I must have seemed an uninspiring—if devoted—wife, and probably a suffocating one too, a 'non-person'. It certainly wasn't a balanced partnership. I needed him so much for my survival that I couldn't attend to his real needs, or perhaps even afford to admit he had any, so no wonder he looked elsewhere! I can see now that he couldn't have really explained all this at the time, even if he knew it clearly in his own mind, because he would have been afraid of destroying me. And no wonder I was so devastated when he made his announcement. For months I went on blaming him for ruining my life!

I've learned all this about myself through getting over it, but I certainly didn't know much about my own dependency at the time. More's the pity. Having to survive all this has certainly made me a richer, more whole person, but I got there the hard way!

Getting on with your life as an agent of your own destiny rather than as a victim of your circumstances does not of course guarantee that your relationship will last. But being able to do this will mean you are far more likely to successfully negotiate the ongoing adjustments that are always necessary for lasting and fulfilling relationships. You will also be far better able to cope with disappointments when they happen to you at the hands of others. It's almost as if, paradoxically, *you need to feel sufficiently self-aware to manage without relationships to be able to function well within them.* You cannot go forward successfully in a relationship unless you can function without one. At the same time, an important part of self-awareness is knowing how significant and necessary relationships are for all of us. So we need to formulate a self-determined life plan which doesn't demand relationships or exclude them. Only then can we master the complex task of interweaving our own needs for separateness and connectedness with those of another person.

Dependency tends to cause communication difficulties from the beginning of a relationship. This is because while you were becoming dependent in childhood, part of protecting your relationship with your caretakers meant suppressing your own emotionality. If expressing anger, aggression, helplessness, fear etc. was not handled well by the important people in your life, perhaps because they don't express their own such feelings, you would quickly have denied yours, and never become knowledgeable about your emotional self. You depended on others to define your emotional self for you. You bring this into adult relationships and are unable to express yourself authentically to your partner. They are therefore unable to relate to a real you. What's more, you will seek to hang on to relationships because you need a source of definition. This causes you to suppress your emotional self still further because you think this self-denial enables you to dedicate yourself to serving your partner's needs. Then they will stay with you because you give so much. You'll tend to let problems that arise be resolved either by always asserting yourself, or by always backing down. You need a sense of dominance to feel real, and to sustain the relationship by controlling it. Submission in its own way serves to control interactions, because it allows dominance.

You must strive to build into your way of relating an ability to solve issues together, without either of you always needing to win or to lose, as early on as possible in your acquaintance. The longer you avoid working at sharing issues as they come up, approaching them as joint challenges rather than as awkward problems, the harder it'll be to change tacks later, when a dominating or submissive pattern has become the habitual way you deal with issues.

People fortunate enough to be in relationships that work are good at solving problems without either person losing out. It isn't that they don't have any problems. Two people cannot solve things together satisfactorily for both of them in the longer term unless both have a reasonably well-defined sense of self. Otherwise your need to assert your point of view—or to deny it—will cause competitiveness, which will constantly generate arguments. Tension and reactivity creep in when either person is having difficulty adjusting to the separateness they each must have, and allow for a productive life to resume for each of them, after the intense interdependency of the initial stage of a relationship. Dependent people cannot make these adjustments satisfactorily because they continue to need to be merged with their partner, to be defined by them.

When you feel submerged in your relationship, it is because you feel unable to assert your 'self' without creating tensions or conflict. This happens either because your self-esteem is low (I don't deserve to have my own opinions and feelings and I'm not sure what they are anyway), or because you know your partner's is (I must protect my partner, she's too fragile to take my assertion on this one). It's only when you are both able to be your own self most of the time, and know when your ordinary dependency is operating, that you really go forward in a relationship and enjoy true intimacy with a sense of real freedom.

Learning more about your relationship needs

We may be discovering more about dependency and poorly-defined selves, and how they affect our relationships, but how do we find out what our relationship needs really are? Many people don't know what they are without experiencing more than one kind of relationship.

Relationship issues are never clear-cut and real certainty is seldom possible. *Armed with increased knowledge and insight, in the end you must go with what you feel.* Don't be afraid to take plenty of time exploring the relationship before making a commitment. Try to address the following points frankly, but don't expect to be able to fully answer them. They are designed to help you check how much your dependency and self-esteem are governing your decision-making:

- How much of an investment do I have in finding a permanent relationship, and could my strong need for one be blinding me to what this person is really like?
- Could my hopes be affecting the way I behave with this person so that quite often I'm not saying what I really think, or not behaving according to what I really believe in? Put another way, the question is 'How much am I being guided by this person to be like I think they'd like me to be rather than like I really am?'
- To what extent am I being influenced by how I think other people outside this relationship (family, friends, even my own children) feel about it? We can subtly be affected by others either seeming to approve and encourage the partnership, or disapprove of it. Only you can make a decision to go into a relationship further, although many of us use the apparent guidance of others to help make our decisions, sometimes without realising it.
- Have I really considered all the possible complications of getting involved with this person and whether I can live with them? Things like your pasts, cultural differences, potentially incompatible career and family ambitions, age gaps, future step-children, and the characteristics of your respective families of origin. Could I be denying the importance of these issues because I want the relationship so much?
- Am I attracted by this different relationship only because I think I'm dissatisfied with my present one? Do I need another relationship to make my decision about my marriage instead of confronting the real issues about what's wrong with it?

You need to address these sorts of things in your own mind, as well as trying to discuss them together. None of them are necessarily in themselves obstacles to the relationship lasting, but not understanding what they mean to you both or ignoring them altogether may turn out to be a problem further down the track.

If all this sounds so cautious and deliberating that you're afraid you might never make a decision about a relationship, or you're too busy analysing the pros and cons to be spontaneous together, remember this: addressing real questions about yourself and your needs is important and can be done without compromising that light-hearted enjoyment vital to a happy relationship. It doesn't mean forgetting to laugh at yourself and your uncertainties! Risks and uncertainties are part of the stimulation and challenge of lively relationships.

If you're reading this while you're in the middle of sorting out what to do about a relationship that's probably going to end, you'll react by thinking, 'I didn't consider any of this when we first got together', and perhaps 'If I had, I'd never have made a commitment'. Regrets about the past are opportunities for useful learning. Understanding what people do and don't do early on in a relationship may be too late now, but it will help you come to terms with what went wrong and equip you with useful knowledge for the future.

What is this thing called selfhood?

We've seen how the problem of having a limited sense of self is not so much not having one, but not knowing about it or how it affects you. Here's what you're aiming for, so you can start to look at whether you have difficulties in expressing your real self. A healthy sense of self involves:

- Having a considered and balanced knowledge of your strengths and weaknesses.
- Having a good grasp of your beliefs and values so that you can articulate them with certainty, and know when you need to do this. It also includes actually living according to the values and beliefs you think you have, and knowing their relative importance to you.
- Understanding the consequences of your standpoint on important issues, and accepting the responsibility you have for them.
- Being able to be emotionally connected to your partner even when there is tension between you, rather than withdrawing into being distant and suppressing your point of view, without making it clear to your partner that you're doing this.

- Being able to present your differences about issues at the same time as allowing your partner to do this too. In other words, you are able to be different without backing down about something you believe in, or always needing to win your partner over to your point of view.
- Being able to discuss difficult and uncomfortable topics and express your position about them.

If you do most of these things with your partner most of the time, or at least realise when you don't and can go back together and have another go, then your relationship is healthy.

Putting a stronger self into practice

The first thing any partner to a relationship they want to last must do is to make a commitment to attending to it. Good marriages don't just happen, they need nurturing. To do this successfully, you need to look after yourself and your own development first, because unless you do you won't be able to hold your own in a relationship and offer it interest as well as get what you want from it. This means regularly reviewing what you want from life, and accepting what is realistic to expect out of a relationship. You must be reasonably happy with yourself and your life most of the time to be able to offer to a relationship something worth having.

Consider how dependent on being married and being a parent you are. Don't expect to be able to answer this question definitely of course, but remember, your partner could always be run over tomorrow even if they don't walk out on you. Your children could die, too. While this sounds morbid, you need to understand your dependency on your role in relation to other people, an issue which is perhaps harder for women to consider. They tend to spend a lot of their lives helping other people to grow and achieve, often at the expense of their own development. This makes them especially vulnerable to loss, and out of touch with their own uniquely individual creative potential, that 'something' which everybody has, and which not everybody develops. It's the one thing that you have that's your own and is in your control. Not only does developing it give you resources to cope with loss, which we all must face sometime, but it makes you a more interesting and respect-worthy partner, and in that sense perhaps one less likely to be left. Here are some suggestions for using selfhood constructively.

- Get something going for yourself that's your very own interest which makes you feel personally satisfied.
- Initiate something surprising and fun with your partner often, and try to get them to do this too.
- Question what options you really have to change things you don't like about your lifestyle. Try and share your ideas with your partner. Talk about changing things just for variety, too.
- Pay attention to the sexual side of your relationship. Acknowledge that this is hard for most people to do, and keep communicating about it.
- Be careful that your worthy commitment to parenting or work hasn't excluded your partner so they feel lonely and out of touch with you. Think of ways to bring more affection into the relationship.

Dependency makes you vulnerable to loss. Don't assume anything could never happen to you, but not so that you live with a pessimistic outlook. If you're trying to communicate regularly with your partner, you're more likely to see the warning signs in time to act on them. This is a much better position to be in than pretending that everything's fine, while letting things slide. If your partner tells you it's over, the chances are you've been kidding yourself that the relationship is okay, and if you're really honest it's probably not a complete surprise. If it's happened to you and the news really is an absolutely shocking surprise, then remember, people don't have to be actors or insensitive psychopaths to effectively cover up things they don't want to face because they're too hard. You haven't been *deliberately* deceived. Your partner has probably gone through considerable anguish about the relationship without being able to tell you. One-sided breakups do happen even though they're incredibly cruel. Your partner may think they've tried to talk to you but feels they got nowhere and gave up. How receptive were you really? Don't assume they haven't also been tormented in their own way by their dilemmas.

All relationships contain two different sets of needs and feelings, including uncertainties, frailties, anxieties, needs for solitude and separateness etc. Getting to know about all of these is a continuous and developing process. Don't make the mistake of thinking that when your relationship begins to change and issues which aren't easy to discuss come up, that something has gone wrong, just because you don't remember having any problems to begin with.

It's easy to confuse dependency with love. Falling in love is very like it, because classically we feel the loved person has made our life worthwhile, has taken away our problems, given our life meaning etc. If you rely on another to do this for any length of time, sooner or later your relationship will be in trouble.

The way dependency and love are interlinked is very complex. Here's a checklist to help you understand how dependency may be affecting your relationship.

- We all need relationships.
- We often marry when we don't know much about ourselves and our needs.
- An undeveloped self can propel us into marriage for the wrong reasons, with dependency and love often getting mixed up.
- Dependency, self-esteem and selfhood are learned in our families of origin, from infancy onwards.
- Dependency is often denied or misunderstood and can put enormous pressure on relationships.
- You should try to consider how much your dependency may be affecting how accurately you appraise relationships.
- You can see how well your relationship is doing by looking at how able you are to express your real self with your partner.
- You need to distinguish between opportunities to meet your dependency needs better, and the attraction of alternative relationships.
- Your self-esteem and dependency are the key to how you react to falling in love, the subject of chapter 2.

Only you can provide your life with meaning. Your unique self must have an existence on its own. Good relationships are about wanting what's best for another person—your partner, your child or your friend—whether or not this suits you, rather than wanting them to modify their behaviour for you. It involves detachment and an ability to allow freedom, independent of your own hopes or expectations. Only then can you embark on the experience of falling in love with vision as well as joy.

2 What is love?

> When I first met her we had wonderful times together. Everything was just perfect. But over the years the magic seems to have gone out of our relationship. The things that attracted me to her don't seem to be so exciting to me any more. It's not that the relationship is all that bad, she's a nice person, and I really have nothing to complain about. It's just got rather dull and I wonder now whether I have outgrown her, because I feel I've progressed a lot with my life. And I do feel attracted by the idea of an affair. Perhaps this is really all there is to marriage after a while.

Parts of this story will be familiar to many of us. What is this feeling called love we all seem to be looking for, enjoying or struggling with? Can it really provide lasting happiness? Most of us who once fell in love want to know what happened to that old magic we used to have, whether it can be recaptured, and whether a new experience with a seemingly more exciting partner means a longstanding relationship is worn out.

The most important question you must address if you're contemplating a change or trying to understand your partner's change of heart is *what is love for me*? The very word 'love' has always had countless different meanings. This in itself implies that we associate love with uncertain, elusive and therefore sought-after qualities. Most of us expect to have and sustain a certain kind of feeling called 'love' in marriage relationships. Understanding more about romantic love is essential to begin finding out how you experience 'love' in primary relationships, and whether this is enough for you. We'll start with a look at the history of love in mate selection.

Romantic love in history

The ideal of romantic love has been recorded in all the world's great literature and mythology from ancient times, and first came into ordinary Western consciousness in the Middle Ages. It was first conspicuously documented in our literature with the story of Tristan and Isolde, and of Lancelot and Guinevere in the Arthurian legends, and became a central theme in mythology, love poems and troubadour songs. In these medieval times its form was 'courtly' love—courtly in the sense of being enacted with dignity, adoring flattery, chivalrous manners and high-mindedness.

Medieval romantic relationships were idealised, exclusive and extramarital, and not usually sexual except in fantasy, though almost always heterosexual. They were believed to be the result of some supernatural force or agent external to the individual such as a love potion (Tristan and Isolde) or an ancient mythical identity (Cupid's arrow). Shakespeare of course further immortalised romantic love with his characters Romeo and Juliet.

The essential features of romantic love were feelings and experiences which passed beyond the limits of ordinary life. This is thought to be why sexuality was too earthly to be part of it. It had the power to heal, to create spiritual wholeness and give immortality. It inspired great adventures, acts of great danger, risk and courage, and directed a person's energy and effort with urgency and single-mindedness. The loved person was attributed with qualities of godlike perfection, and when achieving union with the loved one was thwarted or unrequited, death or lifelong celibate seclusion often followed.

Against this historical background of idealised relationships involving ecstasy, spiritual transcendence, personal sacrifice and tragedy, marriage itself was quite a different matter. Until the end of the nineteenth century romance in Western culture was predominantly by arrangement. Social and family position, reproductive promise, economics and politics determined mate selection. This system served the purpose of sustaining the current social order of a community or society. The function of marriage as a stabilising unit in society depended on the subordinate status of women, an authoritarian and hierarchical social order and limited personal freedom.

Another kind of arranged marriage which remains prevalent in third-world cultures is the bartered marriage. The man purchases a wife whose job it is to rear children and keep house. She has neither rights nor property, and can be replaced by sale. Arranged marriages remain the dominant form of marriage in the non-Western world.

It's only in modern Western society that we have merged romantic love (and all its hopes and hurts) with marriage relationships. Historians generally agree that the love marriage started to evolve somewhere about the sixteenth century. During the Renaissance and Reformation, marriage gradually ceased to have such a necessary role in social ordering because democratic institutions came into being, along with a new consciousness of individual rights, and the very beginnings of a change in status for women. With the relative freedom of post-Renaissance Western society came a new focus on marriage as a source of personal satisfaction. This came about because consciousness started to be governed by more personal and subjective forces rather than by objective, social and even supernatural ones.

When you think about it, the key features of love which have been handed down to us in history and culture substantially remain with us. Features such as passion, ecstasy, a belief that love conquers all, a desperate and compelling quality, a dependence on it for a sense of power, energy, spiritual meaning etc. Whilst our thinking has advanced so we attribute 'falling in love' to some set of subjective, psychological and unconscious forces, we carry with us the expectation of the experience as longlasting, energising and even capable of transcending the ordinary. We still tend to regard it as a goal of life in itself and have idealised hopes for perfect relationships. Falling in love is an experience we often describe as happening to us almost as if we can't help it, as if it is an experience we're powerless but willing victims of. Combined with a long-term commitment to marriage and a sexual relationship, the myths of romantic love—particularly the expectation of lasting ecstasy—can lead us into all sorts of disappointments. *Expectations about romance handed down to us from earlier in our history, which we may not think we are aware of (having never consciously thought about them) have a subtle bearing on what we expect to feel and experience today.*

Modern interpretations of romantic love

History can tell us a good deal about the experience of romance and love, about our expectations of it, and about what social changes over the years have done to alter our thinking about where the experience springs from. Whilst we now generally acknowledge that it is a subjective experience, this doesn't necessarily mean we behave as if it's within our conscious control.

We may think we've had freedom of choice in mate selection since post-medieval times, but have we really? We may not be governed by things like social hierarchy, inheritance, breeding capacity, etc. No longer are our partnerships determined by how many cows we can offer, the size of a dowry, whether two nations should become allies etc., but by a prospective partner's ability to provide psychological satisfaction of our specific emotional needs. It's now our private and subjective world that arranges our marriages, rather than the objective social world. We select our partners by unconscious arrangements according to a partner's value. Unconscious that is, in the sense of outside our everyday awareness. We experience this as a specific and sexually influenced response to another person which seems to just happen as if it was 'meant to be', and in that sense 'arranged' out of our everyday awareness.

Social psychologists, biologists, historians, anthropologists and therapists have put forward all sorts of different theories about the powerfully delightful, yet often painful experience of falling in love. All of the theories offer something to our understanding, and therefore can contribute useful perspectives on relationship dilemmas.

There's the 'evolutionary' explanation, which holds that being attracted by a beautiful or handsome person has survival value to the species as a whole. When we're 'in love' we certainly idealise our loved one's physical characteristics, and admiring them propels us into passionate sexual highs with (at least theoretically!) reproductive results. Men are drawn to women who are attractive, who are admired for their healthy bright eyes, good skin, beautiful hair, youth etc., and anticipated sexuality. A healthy and therefore physically strong mate will provide good fruitful sex and housekeeping energy. Women are drawn to qualities associated with physical strength and dominance over others because of their need to be provided for. Youth in males isn't so highly valued because it isn't so essential to their reproductive ability. Male success and hence attractiveness in fact often increases with age.

A potential partner's evolutionary value doesn't have much bearing in today's world, even though image and presentation, associated as they are with material success, have such a powerful hold on us in our culture. Few of us have reproductive possibilities very much on our minds when we feel drawn to someone, though we may often have sexual pleasure fairly close to uppermost! A woman's youth and appearance, and a man's power and social status undoubtedly do play a big part in attraction. A long time ago these qualities were obviously essential to individual as well as species survival, but there must be more to it than matters of biology and species survival nowadays.

Another explanation proposes that as well as physical attractiveness we are drawn towards a person's character. More specifically we are attracted when we discover we have things in common with a person. Many of us remember the excitement of getting to know someone when interests or attitudes in common unfold between you. You feel a self-affirming sense of oneness which propels you into a relationship. Any slight deficiencies there may be in youth and attractiveness are outweighed by merits of character, accounting for matches between people noticeably different in age or looks. When we first meet we respond almost instantly to a set of appearance and character cues about a person which tells us there are possibilities here. We can call this the equality theory. If we are fairly similar we may be able to have an equal and balanced relationship. This concept has a more contemporary appeal as most of us nowadays think we want freedom and equality in our relationships. In unequal relationships where one partner feels inferior and the other feels superior, guilt, insecurity and anger may interfere with successful development together.

The apparent attraction of opposites can be partly explained by complementarity. Here the idea is that people are attracted by characteristics they see as making up for or balancing their own deficiencies. A partnership broadens the range of possibilities for either person on their own because strengths and talents are pooled, providing a sense of strength and security. If you don't have a skill or quality you wish you did have, the next best thing is to have a mate who does. You quite often hear people cheerfully describing their relationship in terms of complementary qualities.

> Stan and I make a really good team. He's rather quiet socially, the thoughtful intellectual kind, whereas I'm chatty and gregarious. He says he likes this, and being out with me socially makes him feel proud of me and comfortable with what he calls my 'good interpersonal skills'. I once asked him if he felt unmanly always taking the quieter position, but he likes it because he says it gives him time to have important thoughts about people. He's also a really good household administrator and keeps everything really well-organised. I'm hopeless in that area. I don't mind shopping and cooking, but I'm forgetful and casual about record-keeping and budgeting. Thank goodness for our differences!

Yet another idea is that we are driven more or less consciously to attach ourselves to partners we feel are good for the image of ourselves we wish to project. We select a mate who will enhance our self-image, whom others will think is a good catch, who will make people think more of us because we've attracted and held the attention of this admired, eccentric or controversial person. We are able to feel good because we are making a statement about ourself through how our partner is seen by others. We undoubtedly are social beings, influenced by what other people think.

You may react to some of these ideas with a 'yes, that's me', or 'that was definitely us' and gain a new perspective. Perhaps bits of all of them make some sense for some people. But given that each of us crosses paths with physically attractive, characteristically similar, complementary and status-giving potential partners numerous times in our lives, none of these explanations really account for why we picked the person we did; or why some people go headlong into a relationship of intense urgency and ecstasy from first sight, while others start off gradually as friends and move towards marriage at a relatively measured pace; or why we are so often puzzled by what seems to be an attraction of opposites.

For relationship counsellors, the problem with all of them is that whilst they may give you a better understanding of what might have happened or what to look out for, they don't on their own explain why so many relationships become troubled, or generate any starting points for managing relationships better. Neither do they account for the intensity and urgency many of us feel when we've fallen in love; the sense of being 'carried away', as if the experience is beyond our immediate control. The picture of romantic attraction they give is therefore too simple. We have to look further into the subjective experience of love and all its common themes, and study why people describe the same kinds of experiences of falling in and out of love over and over again.

Looking deeper into the romantic marriage

As well as the above difficulties, several other common features of love suggest that something deeper in our unconscious lives must be at work.

First, there's the fact that the idea of love pervades our culture and has existed in some form since ancient times. It affects all the needs and drives of adult life in some way or another for almost every one of us. Its well-known themes abound in our everyday language, our literature and throughout the music and drama of our performing arts.

Second, there's the sheer unmistakable power of the feeling, the sense that we can't help it, it's beyond our control. And the universal similarities in its subjective experience. We feel swept off our feet, we report love at first sight, we are preoccupied with thoughts of the loved person and the relationship. We refer to being 'lovesick', we say or sing things like 'I can't live without you' as if we believe life will be impossible if we lose our loved one. We laughingly excuse the changed behaviour of a friend saying 'they can't help it, they're in love!'. We think we've found a meaning for life at last, a sense of only feeling complete and whole because of the loved one, a sense of a power found only together which makes anything possible, a feeling of having discovered happiness at last etc., etc.

Third, there's the tendency to fall in love with fundamentally similar kinds of people. If you look back on your relationship history it's more than likely you'll discover that you tend to get involved with similar kinds of people, similar in pluses as well as minuses. You mightn't think they're that similar to begin with, and you may even have consciously looked for someone different, but it's surprising how often people find their partners turning out to be similar again and again.

> I remember being quite puzzled not long after my second marriage to find myself starting to call my partner by my first wife's name. It was unfortunate for her and we tried to laugh it off, but the odd thing was I thought I'd got over her years ago. I'd made a resolution with myself not to make a commitment to anyone else until I felt sure I'd left those hurt and angry feelings about my failed marriage behind, so to find myself doing this was really a surprise. It coincided with some of the bloom wearing off this relationship as of course we knew it had to. We'd both had our disappointments and we were determined to put more effort into keeping this relationship alive for good. But one morning I woke up after a rather restless night to a devastating realisation that in all sorts of ways I hadn't realised till then, June was quite like my first wife! Discovering this so disturbed me because I thought I'd found a refreshingly different kind of relationship, that I withdrew into myself for a few weeks. This didn't help the relationship of course but fortunately we were able to bridge the distance and get close again, though I'm still not sure what those similarities really mean about me.

The common themes and feelings of love, and the tendency to fall for basically similar partners do mean something, and are important clues to unravelling the real mystery of romantic attraction.

A deeper interpretation which has helped psychologists and relationship therapists takes as a starting point the links between an individual's experience of being parented and how they subsequently manage adult love relationships. After all, our experience of relationships began with our very earliest ones, those in our family of origin. To explain this framework for understanding the experience of love we must take another look at childhood in rather the same way as we did for understanding dependency. You will discover the very close links between the search for selfhood, the drive to indulge dependency and the force of romantic passion when you observe that some of what you're about to read seems to be similar to some of what we've said in Chapter 1.

From the moment of birth onwards a child depends on their main caretaker to meet all their needs. They must be fed, warm, clean and physically close. They have no conscious awareness of themselves as separate from their caretaker or from the rest of the world. They have in fact no boundaries, and so (as far as we can really know with a newborn infant), they experience for a time a sense of oneness with the rest of the world.

With time every infant experiences some limitations in the efficiency with which their needs are met—no parent is perfect—and so begins to develop a sense of their own self through the experience of their needs sometimes being met inadequately. Later still, the child's natural instinct to express the full energy of their real as yet untamed self, and their characteristic sense of their own omnipotence, must be contained because of their almost complete dependence on their parents. All parents have their own individual approach to caretaking. They vary in how protective and restraining they are, how encouraging of independence; how much they limit and guide their child's expressions of feelings, emotions and sexuality; how much they control the socialisation and moral training of their child.

We have all (certainly those of us who are parents) marvelled at the sheer unrestrained vitality and exuberance of small children, and delighted in their spontaneous energy and raw enthusiasm, perhaps even envied it! Certainly at times we've been exhausted by it. Gradually, in order to mature and integrate into their world, every child's natural self and its expression must be contained and disciplined in ways which parents are substantially in control of. For a time children continue to express their energy and sense of omnipotence in their play and in fantasy, another marvel for us restrained adults to behold! To a greater or lesser extent then, depending on our parents' approach to rearing us and our other experiences, all of us grow up with parts of our natural selves suppressed, undeveloped or denied, but which nevertheless continue to exist in our unconscious minds.

Many psychologists believe that it is a powerful drive to recover the lost or suppressed parts of ourselves that causes us to fall in love with such force, pursuing the exciting sense of wholeness and great potential we feel in love. We are attracted, so they say, to certain combinations of positive and negative characteristics which closely match those of our parents. This happens so that we can recreate the conditions of our childhood within which, because of our dependency and our experience of being parented, we lost the struggle to express and refine our unique sense of self. A certain kind of partner gives us the opportunity to win the struggle for a sense of wholeness this time around. It is the very similarities of the loved object to our parents and therefore to the conditions of our childhoods that gives us that instant glimpse once more of our childhood wholeness and energy that's long since been lost. This sense we experience in love of having transcended the ordinary, achieved extraordinary vitality and a meaning for life at last, therefore has more to do with our own incompleteness as a person since early childhood, than with the real merits or long-term suitability of our loved one.

A simpler way of putting this idea that we re-enact our childhood experiences in marriage is to describe love relationships as providing opportunities for accomplishing specific developmental tasks. Although many of us don't remember very much about our childhoods, our early years form the emotional blueprint for our adult lives. We search to understand ourselves better through close relationships with others, we use them to seek more perfect self-definition, to solve emotional issues such as our sexuality, self-sufficiency, creativity; or to come to terms with emotions we don't manage very well like anger, sorrow or aggression. Through relationships we both give and take much needed assistance with self-discovery. We all have emotional sorting out to do, and relationships provide the adult setting for this necessary task.

The problem with adult love-partnerships is that another person cannot provide anything other than a temporary and illusory sense of wholeness. To begin with we do a lot of giving in order to please and gratify our loved one. This makes us present to them a false picture of our own emotional competence, an apparent lack of neediness and an endless capacity to give. With time of course our own individual needs must break through and we each begin to demand more from the other, more separateness as well as more gratification of our real needs. When this enjoyable illusion of romance subsides we tend to react with the same resentment and frustration as we did as a child when our needs weren't met.

We demand things and accuse our 'caretaker' of having withdrawn their love, of having changed, and we protest loudly.

A readjustment of our expectations of adult partnerships, and a better understanding of how our unconscious minds operate is necessary so that we can adjust better through the transition from the early phase of love. Only then can we achieve a balance together which enables us to pursue our own development with the aid of the relationship while retaining our own separateness.

Two people cannot necessarily pursue their developmental tasks at a jointly workable pace. If we succeed at completing some of our developmental tasks we may find the relationship no longer serves us because we have outgrown it. If we do not manage to get in touch with what we need to do for ourselves in relationships, we'll find we repeat our characteristic patterns of functioning in future partnerships.

Relationship counsellors have found that exploring a person's experience of being parented provides great insight into the unconscious issues they bring with them into adult relationships. Bringing these issues into conscious awareness has been shown to be an effective way of improving marriage relationships.

Exploring your relationship history

It may come as a surprise that ideas that exist in our folk-lore about relationships, such as people marrying a replica of their parent of that sex, in fact have come to have some credibility and usefulness. You may find the idea of re-enacting your childhood in marriage a bit far-fetched and speculative. Or you may feel the beginnings of an uncanny sense of fit about it. Perhaps you'll be intrigued enough to want to investigate the idea further, through your own reading or thinking, or in psychotherapeutic counselling. If you're curious, try having some fun with this exercise:

Part 1: Rediscovering your early relationships

- Position yourself comfortably somewhere you won't be interrupted for half an hour or so.
- Think back to your childhood and try to recapture some of the physical settings of it.

- Identify in your mind the people most important to you in the various stages of your early life.
- Remember what you most liked about these people, and what you didn't like about them.
- Recall what you remember wanting from them and whether you got these things or not.
- Write down all this information about your experience of being parented.

Part 2: Examining your current relationship

- Make a list of five of your partner's qualities which first attracted you to the relationship.
- Make another list of five things you value about your partner now.
- Now list a further five things you'd rather were different or weren't there at all.

Part 3: Connecting past with present

- Compare what you have written down for Parts 1 and 2, and look for any links or common themes between your two sets of jottings.
- Try and work out what this analysis might mean about what you want from a relationship.

Falling in love and selfhood

Let's now move on from these intricacies of unconscious needs, conflicts and desires. Where you actually lost your wholeness of self along the way to adulthood, or how you came to have a limited one is interesting and potentially illuminating. But we must get on with accepting in more everyday terms what actually happens, so we can get on with doing something about it. In the midst of all this analysis, we wouldn't want to lose sight of the sheer delights of being in love, and its value in ensuring we get hitched up to someone! Without it relationships might never get started!

Whatever you make of the idea of a suppressed unconscious being brought into marriage, one thing's certain: *a reasonably robust sense of self and an awareness of how this self of yours functions is essential to a workable relationship.* We saw this in Chapter 1 and now we need to know more about how selfhood interacts with the experience of love in particular ways. It's worth reconsidering this important point because it's so central to why relationships go wrong.

When we feel unable to assert ourselves with a dominant partner, the frustration we experience is our separate selves struggling to exist. When we feel disappointed in our partner's apparent inertia or neediness, we are often experiencing discomfort at being depended on too much, or at having to be too directive, supportive or motivating for them. Many of us have felt suppressed or contained by a relationship and have struggled to be free of it, unable to feel free within it. So we have felt the importance of selfhood. In spite of this we seldom really notice—let alone do anything about it in our marriages—the impossible demands we make when we use a relationship with another person to make us feel whole and energised. Another person cannot make you into a complete individual. When you ask this of a partner you will generate frustrations for yourself and your partner.

Underneath all the happiness and anticipation of a new relationship there are hidden traps for those of us who aren't in touch with our selves. The stage is already set for a mistaken belief that relationships happen automatically. We get delightfully caught up in the excitement of falling in love and everything seems rosy. The magic of romantic love has energy of its own, a 'chemistry' which makes us behave as if the relationship doesn't need any effort. The new feeling of sexual and emotional fulfilment combined with the sense of discovery and companionship is so exciting it just seems to flow and progress. Satisfaction is immediate and exists just because of the relationship.

What we aren't usually aware of is that we are each presenting to the other at this time an illusory impression of our own infallibility. We want to give and do so much to please the other that we appear to have no needs of our own. Our own needs and frailties are disguised so that our partner invests us with qualities we don't in fact have. The passion of being newly 'in love' subsides as we get on with everyday life together. The love period of a new relationship is time-limited and lasts from a few months to about two and a half years. Time passes and the mundane catches up with us. Our real and incomplete selves must re-emerge. The qualities that were disguised are only then revealed, causing us to conclude that our partner has actually changed.

When we reach this point we may mistakenly think that the relationship has gone wrong because it seems to have changed. Unfortunately (but understandably) we often keep these confused doubts to ourselves because it feels too hard to discuss them. We want to hang on to the intense feelings that seem to be able to override obstacles. The very fact that the relationship didn't seem to need any effort at first makes it feel threatening to start talking about problems, doubts and unsatisfied needs. Issues of life and of sharing seem to feel like problems rather than challenges because we've so far relied on the strong positive feelings to just take care of everything. We fall into the trap of not speaking our minds and avoiding facing issues together.

Another danger of new love is that we quickly become so afraid of losing the relationship that makes us feel whole and gives meaning to our life that we start to 'gloss over' or disregard aspects of the relationship that we're uncomfortable about. Uncertainty and fear of losing the relationship is the part of falling in love that makes it all so urgent and consuming. We do indeed want to hang on to this precious thing and reassure ourselves continually of its magic by indulging in it. We start to do things, say things and even think things to please our loved one, to ensure their interest. We make compromises we aren't aware of about our own needs and feelings so as to preserve the partnership. How many times have you reflected on an exchange with a lover to realise that you didn't say what you really felt at all? Here is another way that communication patterns begin which later on become unsatisfactory and frustrating.

> Mike and I had been together for a glorious six months when things started to change a bit. We were both feeling very positive about the relationship. On the few days we didn't see each other we'd talk for ages at night on the phone. These talks would finish up with Mike sounding a bit frustrated and impatient increasingly often, but I never really knew why. Next day when we were together it was all marvellously romantic again so it didn't occur to us to address what had happened the night before. It was as if we'd forgotten it had happened. The intensity of our feelings seemed to

> be able to override these small uncertainties. Several months later Mike said he wanted to have a break and think about the relationship. I was very disturbed by this because it seemed so sudden. I had no idea why he would want to withdraw when the times we had were so good. Much later I realised that those good times were preventing me seeing what was really going on, and that these uncertainties I felt about our talks probably weren't small. I was wanting the good times to continue so much that I wasn't really being myself. Even if I had let myself see these warning signs I don't think I'd have dared bring them up in case it destroyed the relationship.

We have begun to see that the emphasis we place on romantic love as the basis for mate selection has a lot to answer for. It makes us expect too much from and do too little for relationships in the longer term. It makes us ill-equipped for the transition from romance to real relationship. It makes us inclined to think companionate love is dull and ordinary by comparison, and makes us vulnerable to the apparent attractions of another relationship which seems to be able to give us those intense feelings again.

When we contemplate a long-term partnership we hope to feel a deep sense of lasting commitment as thrilling in its way as being newly in love. But many people find themselves unable to adapt to changes caused by the dimming of romantic passion. They cannot adjust to significant events like the arrival of children, financial pressures, career moves, personal ambitions and other potential stresses. They have relied on the passion of love to automatically take care of all challenges, and when dissatisfactions arise they tend to mistakenly blame the relationship for them. They find it more difficult to make the necessary compromises and adjustments than they would if they had a more realistic idea of long-term partnerships, and a better understanding of themselves in relationships. Like Mike above they may terminate the relationship as soon as it seems to be changing.

Falling in love is always temporary. No matter who we fall in love with the honeymoon always ends, the ecstatic lovingness subsides because two separate selves each with their own true strengths and weaknesses must reappear. This needn't mean we stop loving our partner because they've changed. Once two real selves make up the relationship rather than two idealised lovers, lasting love can really begin. Two real selves have the capacity to generate the interest, affection and challenges for a committed relationship.

Contemporary stresses on the romantic marriage

Nowadays there are other stresses, additional to those arising from misunderstandings about romantic love, which can cause relationships to end up being a disappointment. We tend to ask for very many different things from modern relationships, more than they can possibly provide. We want the freedom to pursue our hopes and dreams, and to grow and develop together as well as individually, unrestricted by traditional stereotypes of male and female roles; to enjoy sexual closeness that is mutually satisfying, as well as stimulating companionship; and we even tend to rely on partnerships to provide personal strength and guidance which we might once more often have drawn from spiritual sources. All this at the same time as seeking status through work in our very achievement-oriented society, running a home, achieving economic security, and raising successful children. The achievement of all these goals for *both* partners—which many of us now aim for—places a great deal of unfair pressure on relationships.

When people's lives were more affected by things like surviving wars, mortality, health, finding food, natural fertility, traditional male/female duties and responsibilities, organised spirituality, and patriotism, than they are now (at least in the affluent Western cultures) there was little room for partners to ask of their relationships the things many of us have now come to want from them. What we expected to give and to get from marriage was more clear-cut. There almost seemed to be a stronger sense of commitment to partner and family in the face of these influences. Substantially released from these directives, our greater contemporary freedom to seek what we individually want from marriage, has given us a sometimes overwhelming range of choices about how we want to experience it, and to depend on relationships to meet more of our personal needs and ambitions than ever.

In a happy partnership where both of you can grow as individuals alongside one another, open and honest communication needs to be there from the beginning. *If you're fortunate enough to have plenty of personal confidence and self-awareness, then your chances of achieving the transition from romance into a longer-term relationship which satisfies you and which lasts, are high.*

Marriages are hardly ever really perfect, but perhaps too often we think they can be and are unwilling to settle for less. Learning to understand what's really happened and is happening in your marriage (including how your unconscious needs are and aren't satisfied) will help you become more self-aware, enabling you to manage your life-after-separation more effectively, and improving your chances of a better relationship next time. Both of you need to put effort into your marriage, it can't survive unattended to for long. The fact is though that most people either don't recognise this, or if they do they don't know how to apply the necessary attention to their relationship. It just feels too hard. Resolutions aren't carried through or are undertaken too late, because the basic commitment from both partners just isn't there.

You need to accept that a relationship must change with time, often leading you to feel a deeper, more stable sense of commitment, with an energy which can be just as satisfying as the magic you felt when you first met, and even more so because this kind of less frantic energy lasts.

Moving from romance to real relationship

Here's a list of some of the things you have to do to successfully navigate the crucial transition from being 'in love' to being in a workable relationship:

- Accept that the price of experiencing the delights of falling in love is bringing a whole range of deceptions into the early period of a relationship.
- Begin communicating your real feelings and needs (including your own confusion about some of them!) to your partner as early on in the relationship as possible.
- Take responsibility yourself for your weaknesses as well as your strengths.
- Accept that there is probably more to the way you operate in a relationship than you may be aware of, and be willing to examine this.
- Be able to allow your partner to have their own needs and feelings, and value them as much as you do your own.

- Understand that your partner cannot provide you with a good relationship just because of who they are. Be aware that this misconception causes you to idealise them. You must cultivate a more accurate picture of your partner. They are just another imperfect human being with needs of their own.
- Accept that creating a good marriage requires courage and effort from both partners, it doesn't just happen.

Romance and separating

It's hard to separate cooperatively from a marriage based on romance. Emotions of a very different, painful kind will interfere with the decision-making and discussion that you both face. All those loving joyful feelings you once had will swing full arc to produce anger, mistrust and sadness. The wholeness and meaning you depended on your partner to provide is threatened, and this causes extreme anxiety and resentment. You blame your partner, because you relied on them (the way you relied for your survival on your parents) to take care of your needs, for having punished you by withdrawing their love. You accuse them (not yourself!) of having changed, and you protest at being abandoned and seek to punish them for their perceived faults.

You planned your future together to begin with, even to the small details like what colour-scheme to have in the bedroom. But you'll most likely find you can't plan to end it together, even though it's a joint failure and should ideally continue to be a joint responsibility.

Separating is really a process rather than an event. You both have to 'disengage' from your life together, and it takes time to adjust to the emotions of it all. This is true for both of you in different ways at different times, however one-sided the decision to separate may have seemed. You may look back on it all later and see that before you parted there was a long period when one of you felt there were problems. Maybe the other didn't want to recognise this, and you couldn't discuss your feelings very productively. This often means that at the time you actually separated you weren't able to jointly prepare yourselves for it because your feelings about parting weren't the same. So it all probably happened in a less than ideal way, because you were understandably preoccupied with your own position. These aspects of separating are linked to our romantic expectations of relationships and are important. We look at this further in Chapter 7.

Romantic marriages are as popular as ever, despite our misleading expectations. We pair up with the same idealised notions of effortless happiness, open communication and assumed fidelity, naturally progressing to a cementing of the relationship through having children. We have the same expectations of lasting happiness that people have had for generations, despite current marriage failure rates.

Making a commitment to a relationship is one of the most exciting and significant decisions of our lives, but we are ill-prepared for anticipating that beyond the 'honeymoon' period, marriages need a mutual commitment to putting in effort. *Understanding romantic love helps us appreciate better that the essentially self-centred elements of passionate love must change to a less dependent, freedom-giving kind of love with time.*

3 Men and women

Apart from being another important aspect of the way we conduct and experience relationships, like selfhood and romantic love, gender and sex have a chapter of their own for two main reasons. Gender means all those things about being either the male or the female in a partnership that make you uniquely different from your opposite-sex partner. However much we might look for equality and sameness in our modern individualistic world, emotionality, needs, ambitions, sensitivity and sexuality for example, are significantly different for men and for women. Whether these differences are products of inherent gender uniqueness or socialised expectations is a matter of continuing popular and scientific controversy. Whatever their origins, they continue to affect the way we conduct our relationships. We want our relationships to allow us equality of opportunity, but we don't always acknowledge or accept that we aren't the same, and this is a frequent source of tension.

Women may want men to become more involved in nurturing and parenting roles, to 'soften' them up and make them more 'feeling'. Men may want women to be more worldly and confident so they can achieve successful careers and be stimulating partners and efficient home-makers. But we can't just reorganise in a matter of a few decades something so fundamental as the basic expectations, feelings and reactions we have in relationships—whatever they stem from—which arise from our opposite gender positions. They have their roots so far back in time that they continue to operate today.

Understanding more about the way males and females tend to

behave in relationships is the first reason for this chapter. If you know more about your partner's general maleness or femaleness, particularly how their gender contributes to the way they express feelings and communicate generally, you may become more accepting, less frustrated and accusing, and make some useful changes as a result.

Nowhere are these differences more acutely focused than in the area of sexual expression, which is the second reason. Dissatisfaction with sex is a major, if not the most important symptom of relationship breakdown. Even today ignorance and misconceptions about sex are surprisingly common, so you shouldn't be leaving a marriage just because your sex life isn't good enough. Don't allow an exciting affair to tempt you to move on unless you've had a long hard look at what you're after, and made serious attempts to examine what isn't working well sexually with your present partner. You may be able to fix it up!

If all this seems too late for this relationship, you'll learn something useful for future ones. Our coverage is an overview of the important issues, enough to start you off with increasing your awareness and skills for gender, sex and relationships.

Some background insights

A look back in time readily reminds us that males have had to be fighters and hunters, and women to be nurturers. In order to succeed men have had to compete, cultivating aggression, physical excellence and even dominance over others. These characteristics have always been essential for survival and this has had two main consequences. Women tended to value, and were therefore attracted to, men who had them. Men developed a tendency to cultivate emotions such as anger and assertion (which were necessary to fighting and achieving) at the expense of expressing other emotions. Women, involved as they were with childbearing and childcare, needed successful providers and protectors. At the same time their role as the primary reproducer of the species and protectors of the young meant they had to be more concerned than men with the day to day business of providing close, nurturing and educating relationships for their young. Men, involved as they were with cultivating skills for protecting and providing couldn't afford to allow themselves to express feelings like hurt and sadness, anxiety and fear because these tended to interfere with the successful performance of their primary tasks.

We left our caves a long time ago, but are things really all that different now? Most of us were children when men were expected to succeed by seeking their fortune, and women by finding and keeping a successful man. Women had work roles and careers of course, but usually spent more time thinking and planning for marriage than they did for work. Although times have changed radically in the last few decades, the priorities for most of us are still the same today. Men strive to feel successful, both as individuals and as eligible mates, largely through the pursuit of work-defined ambitions. In our achievement-oriented and materialistic world, aggression, assertion and dominance are still the important traits for male success. Men still depend on women to provide the tender, intimate and nurturing parts of life that they need but aren't good at attending to. Despite the valuable changes taking place to remove traditional restrictions on equality of access by both men and women to all opportunities, women are still substantially concerned with nurturing and men with achieving outside the domestic arena. Women remain the experts at the nuances of intimate and tender feelings, and remain less expert at showing assertion, anger and aggression. These emotions served no useful purpose to women in the more traditional dominant male/submissive female relationships that used to be more accepted than they generally are now. *But they are necessary for getting what you want, particularly for asserting what you want from your relationship.*

Even in today's dual career families, where the man supports the woman's productivity outside the home, enjoying the extra finance and the stimulation of having a partner with their own challenges, you hear many women remark that they do all or most of the nurturing and home management as well as their work. You only have to listen to young adults chatting socially (say on a bus or train) to notice how groups of girls tend to be talking about their boyfriends, whereas boys are talking about study or sporting interests. Women seem to talk to other women as if their relationships are their priority, as if they define themselves in terms of their partners. Men often seem to be talking to other men about women in the language of successful conquests. Girls, it seems, are still practising their relationship sensitivity, boys mastery of their world outside relationships!

Although scientists are beginning to find out more about real differences between the sexes in brain structure, physiology and genetics, many of us now question the expectations we have of our male and female children. We want to counteract in our parenting the limitations these expectations may place on their future access to opportunities. However much we may want to have our sons grow up more in touch with their feelings, and our daughters to be more upfront and assertive, unwittingly we still tend to do things like comfort and protect our daughters when hurt with more patience and sympathy than we give our sons. We tend to explain events more concretely and with less detail about feeling to our sons than we do to our daughters. Often parents marvel at their sons' tendency to physical play and attraction to action-styled toys, and their daughters' enjoyment of traditionally female play with dolls and nurturing-styled games, despite their own attempts to encourage equality of experience for their children. Even though among adults we may attempt to assert equality of opportunity between the sexes, many of us still have subtly different expectations about the behaviour and priorities of men and women.

What this means in modern relationships

None of this may come as much surprise, but two significant results of this state of affairs are important here. The first is that the differences in the way men and women express themselves emotionally and sexually in relationships, and indeed what they want from them, significantly affect the ongoing course of relationships and separations. For example, it has become commonplace to remark that men aren't good at expressing intimate feelings because they're afraid of being vulnerable, but what isn't so common, unfortunately, is an understanding of how this affects relationships. The second is that nowadays as never before, misunderstood tension frequently exists in relationships. This results from the conflict between what men and women now want and expect from partnerships and their respective differences in communication and emotional expression. Not so long ago, gender differences in emotional and sexual expression were much more manageable, because we accepted more readily the traditional dominance of the male and submissiveness of the female.

One thing we do have more in common than before though, is that we all value satisfying relationships which include good sex. Women acknowledge the importance of good sex more than they did or could admit before. Men value satisfying relationships and real closeness more than they did or could admit before. But while we may be more aware of what we value now, we aren't yet very good at knowing how to get it. This woman's story shows how it is hard for her to find a solution to feeling overstretched in the relationship.

> I was keen to keep up my work skills even while our children were still young, and Kevin encouraged me not to give up work completely, so we got outside help. I assumed that part of what Kevin valued about me was my work achievements. But as time went on I realised that in spite of this he tended to assume that because I was Mum, it'd be me who still ran around organising the gardener, the shopping, the children etc. He didn't seem to be aware of the need for these things to be seen to, but assumed they'd be done. They didn't get done unless I organised them, and I ended up often tired and irritable. When we had tender time together I was always thinking about things that had to be remembered like putting out the cleaning lady's money! He used to try and listen to my point of view on how much of a struggle I felt it was to just keep going, but he didn't seem to be able to contribute to actually helping me. You can guess how much energy I had to enjoy sex! I really think he cares, but it's as if he just can't, because of his maleness, concern himself with domestic matters, or with my diminished sexual affection. He comes home from work needing to be nurtured and provided for, and I want to be able to do this for him. But I need some nurturing too, and the jobs have to be done!
>
> Sometimes I resent the unfairness of the working woman's lot, but I don't think I can blame Kevin, he wasn't brought up to think about household things or to know how to handle feelings like my resentment.

Common areas for conflict in modern relationships

Misunderstood gender factors create the following kinds of situations.

- Men like Kevin respect an individual's right to do their own thing, and so they want a partner who is independently productive outside the traditional domestic field. But they haven't really accepted the consequences of this for the relationship in day-to-day life. Perhaps they feel that their dignity as sole provider is being threatened or undermined; they resent a less than efficiently run household and an exhausted sexual partner. Without realising it, they may behave competitively with their partners over the perceived worth of their respective work achievements. This reflects their inability to relinquish a more comfortable dominant role in the relationship. Again without realising it, they aren't accepting being asked for a greater contribution to housekeeping and parenting activities.
- Women like Kevin's wife want their partner to contribute more to domestic and parenting roles so they are freer to do their own thing, but they resent that this doesn't seem to come naturally. They may enjoy the status, material comforts and security of a partner who is externally successful (he uses assertion, dominance and competitiveness to get success). At the same time they want a closer and communicating kind of relationship with their partner, in which he shows the very things (sensitivity to and skill at expressing fear, sadness, love and intimacy) that are essential to close relationships in families. But he lacks practice at these, having been busy using his other skills for achieving the external success the female partner values him having.
- Men, in keeping with modern ideals of successful women who are more intellectually stimulating companions, want wives who are not just satisfied with being at home and progressively becoming dull, unproductive partners. The woman at home believes she is doing a better job of giving her man what she thinks he wants (a well-run, nurturing and supportive home life with proper priority given to raising the children), than she could if she had her own career/work priorities. He may not be realistic about what having a high-powered partner might actually be like. She may be hiding behind a worthy dedication to nurturing to avoid the personal challenge of performing outside her home role.
- Women tend to blame themselves when there is conflict or when something goes wrong. This may be because of a

deep-seated expectation of dependency on male dominance—sometimes tinged with a fear of their aggression and anger—and also because of their own lack of practice with assertion, and their relative comfort with submission. A woman tends to turn her conflicts in on herself, being more readily in touch with her emotions, and feels inadequate or depressed as a result. Men tend to deal with conflict or problems by placing blame, or expressing anger, outside themselves. This is another example of differences in the emotional currency that is immediately available to men and to women.

- Women want equal relationships based on real intimacy and find themselves frustrated at not being able to 'reach' their partners at an emotional level. Women, as we've seen, have had more practice at articulating the intimate feelings central to close, trusting relationships. Men have had more practice at the 'combat-useful' feelings that are central to competitive relationships. They can't fathom what it is that women are really wanting when the men are providing reliability, a secure income, strength, fidelity, etc. Women complain that their men are emotionally distant. They know all about their man's real needs and feelings (they've had to become good at working it out for themselves!), but can't get them to acknowledge or share them. This means that the challenges of relationships are tackled differently. Men tend to use dominance or withdrawal and are unable to acknowledge real and very relevant feelings like anxiety, fear and uncertainty. Women tend to give in, perhaps with awkward attempts at assertion, and find it impossible to have their expressed feelings taken into account and respected.
- A woman may feel frustrated in a relationship, believing it is holding her back from being herself and going places. She may think it's because her husband isn't interested in facilitating her growth, isn't allowing room for her to make any changes and is wanting things to stay as they are. She feels her needs aren't being attended to. He responds (perhaps without realising it) to what he sees as her need to be nurtured. He wants to provide for and protect her and enjoy things just as they are, not wanting to convey that he wants more from her or for her; not wanting her to feel she should be working, just because it's the modern thing for women to do. Her need for him to be

dominant and the security of the submissive, home-based role this enables her to assume, has distorted into a feeling on her part that he is suppressing her. She is blaming the relationship for her lack of fulfilment, which is a sign of misunderstood dependency. She may dream of another kind of relationship where this doesn't happen, rather than address what is really going on in this one.

- Another kind of relationship impasse results from unacknowledged dependency. If, however subconsciously, you believe that being needy is a weakness, then you are unlikely to acknowledge the contribution your partner is making to the relationship. You cannot see that your partner is giving things like emotional support, nurturing and loyalty, because to do so would involve admitting you needed them. Your partner may feel that what they are giving isn't appreciated. You are likely to see the problems of the relationship in terms of your partner's faults (you're doing all the giving). You're likely to appreciate all the things your partner did give only after the relationship has ended. Men are more likely to deny their needs than women are.
- Many women feel torn by modern expectations of what women should be doing. They find they're saying things to people like 'I'm only a housewife'. No matter how much a woman may be committed to her traditional domestic role, there's no doubt that changing expectations about women are a source of pressure in our achievement-oriented culture. (We've looked at selfhood and the importance of working out what we want in life in Chapter 1. It can be especially difficult for women to do this because domesticity, profoundly worthwhile though it is, tends to foster people-dependency). One of the consequences of this pressure on women is that men feel frustrated in trying to find out what their women really want. They find it hard to deal with their partner's chronic dissatisfaction and ambivalence about themselves and their lives.
- Women tend to be uncomfortable with expressing anger, as we've mentioned. This is mainly because, historically, this expression served no useful purpose while they had no real power to change anything about their relationships and more readily accepted their subordinate position. Even now, when assertion by women has become increasingly necessary and acceptable,

they still tend to express anger by internalising it or withdrawing affection. If she is tense and stand-offish, he assumes she's in a bad mood and leaves it at that, because he's not good at interpreting behaviour. Women tend to respond to anger directed at them by questioning what they've done to deserve it. Subtly this may permit a man, who expresses his anger more outwardly, to let the blame for his anger rest with her where it is allowed to lie. Inappropriately expressed anger creates chronic tension and major barriers to good communication.

- Anxiety is another important emotion that men and women handle differently. Men aren't good at acknowledging they feel anxiety so they cannot make their real needs met or understood. A woman may have to guess that her man is experiencing anxiety in order to give him appropriate support. She is better at expressing her own anxiety, but her man is unlikely to be able to deal with it sympathetically or patiently since he can't deal with his own anxiety very well. Anger and anxiety become especially significant in troubled relationships because they interfere significantly with problem-solving.
- Because men aren't good at expressing emotions like fear, anxiety, sadness and dependency, many avoid acknowledging problems in relationships which inevitably arouse these sorts of feelings. They tend to deny, or at least avoid, the reality of what's happening and find it difficult to address issues or seek help with them. Many women are able to recognise problems and try to do something about them, but find their men unable to join them in doing this. Denial of feelings is a way of avoiding emotional pain. Because addressing real issues always involves some anxiety and discomfort, denial is one way of avoiding opportunities for tackling important issues in a relationship. It's therefore not surprising that men tend to start new relationships instead of addressing what's really happened in their existing one. Many men find themselves taking longer to recover from a breakup than they anticipated. They don't allow themselves to experience painful feelings. Denying them retards emotional recovery (see Chapter 9).

These are just a few of the gender-based problems that frequently crop up in relationships. You'll probably find some of them rather familiar. If you just react to a surface problem with resentment and frustration, you'll never 'reach' each other let alone solve the problem. In a relationship that works, these issues can be examined together and understood for what they really are. Then you can come to accept that men and women have different ways of feeling and communicating. You'll be able to laugh at the knots you tie yourselves in over your different viewpoints, then get on with working out what to do about them. You can begin to change those attitudes and expectations you both agree need adjusting.

The crucial point about emotional expression is that male or female, *we all experience a full range of emotional feelings. They don't disappear because we aren't in touch with them, they are there somewhere in all of us.* Misunderstood, unacknowledged emotions cannot be expressed authentically or communicated accurately, causing inner tensions and resulting relationship difficulties. This, you'll remember from Chapter 1, is an important handicap stemming from a limited knowledge of your real emotional self.

> We reached the stage of having real problems between us. Louise was constantly complaining that the way I was running my life—lots of work and separate sporting activities—didn't demonstrate my commitment and love to her and to the marriage. She felt she was making all sorts of changes and compromises in what she wanted to be doing in order to be with me and support my ambitions, and that I wasn't making any. She was constantly pressuring me to say I loved her, wanted her and would make changes for her, and I found I couldn't. Whatever I tried to do to show that I loved her enough to want her to feel free to do her own thing, she'd twist what I said into my meaning I *didn't* love her, which wasn't what I was saying at all. If I said something like I couldn't see myself settling down traditionally and pushing a supermarket trolley or a stroller, what I meant was I didn't think I was ready to do that yet. She'd come straight back and quote me as having said I never wanted children and so I didn't love her. She seemed to want me to prove I loved her by making the changes she wanted without addressing the real issues, such as why she was blaming all our problems on me. After a while I found I didn't talk to her at all about what was happening between us, because it would always end up with her twisting what I said into a demonstration of my lack of love and

> commitment. It was a real stalemate because, while I accept that the way I'm currently running my life isn't conducive to traditional domesticity, I know I'm not prepared to make real changes yet, and it wouldn't solve anything anyway if I made them just because she demanded them.

This story shows how a woman may turn her anger and disappointment at her partner into feeling inadequate and unloved herself. She showed this by needing frequent reassurances and real demonstrations of her partner's love in the form of his giving up things that were important to him. It shows also how a man may tend to withdraw from potentially helpful communication partly because of his discomfort with facing emotional issues, a need to protect his partner from hurtful realities about the relationship and a need to hang on to his active life outside the domestic arena. Her apparent need for him was itself driving him away. This woman really had made a lot of changes in the interests of supporting her partner's lifestyle, changes which women, because of their different expectations of married life, are often readier to make.

Other gender factors can lead to estrangement rather than conflict. A woman may have done things with her life, grown and changed with experience in ways which threaten her man deep down, because he's really more comfortable with his partner as she used to be. He may distance himself emotionally from her as a way of coping. She may find her needs for a successful, status-giving partner aren't being met if she feels he isn't achieving enough, and this has affected her respect for him and her own sense of security. A man may feel he has worked long hours over the years, while his partner raised the children, and she has become closer to the children than to him. He isn't getting the love and reinforcement from her that he needs. She hasn't had the opportunities or the feelings necessary for her to give him the love and support that he needs, because they haven't been spending enough time together. She has been fulfilling her own needs for closeness through the satisfactions of parenting. He has become lonely in his own family. These factors can all lead to a marriage of parallel separateness with little closeness, and no reason (except habit and a fear of change) for staying together.

Sex

Sex itself is just another gender-based issue which is either a source of satisfying complementarity or eroding conflict. Like any aspect of long-term relationships, it's the source of good experiences as well as not-so-good ones from time to time. As we noted earlier, unsatisfactory sex is a major reason for separating. Inability to deal with sexual incompatibility often stems from communication problems, so really it's all linked together.

Good sex is central to a good relationship and we all want both. In happy relationships, sexual expression is part of this happiness, and sexual satisfaction in turn further enhances relationships. The dovetailing of sex with the rest of a relationship can work like an upward spiral of mutual enrichment.

In the beginning, sex is an automatic part of a new love experience. When we're newly in love we don't need much turning on! But like anything you do often enough, the excitement and instant arousal tends to wear off with time. Many, if not most, couples gradually find they engage in and enjoy sex less and less often. They become increasingly preoccupied with other things and don't expect to have to put any effort into keeping sex interesting. This doesn't necessarily matter (although you're missing out on something that's very positive for your relationship) if the two of you are in synchrony about how often you want and need it. Unfortunately couples often aren't. Everyday problems and preoccupations tend to depress the capacity for sexual satisfaction. Diminished experience of sexual satisfaction tends to worsen everyday problems. This of course is the downward spiral, and it can turn quite quickly into a situation in which the man feels the woman isn't interested enough in him and the woman feels the man doesn't show her enough real love to make her responsive and interested. Sadly, an unattended stalemate like this about the sexual side of a relationship is widespread and is often, along with communication problems extending throughout the relationship, eventually terminal. It certainly makes the attraction of a new and sexually satisfying relationship enticing. The good news is that increased basic knowledge combined with improved communication and committed effort can really be effective in unlocking the stalemate and can dramatically improve sex in long term relationships.

Sex and relationships

Once again we're going to begin by revising our knowledge of the subject to become more informed. So consider these significant issues.

- We tend to expect men to have a stronger, more immediate sex drive, to be more readily aroused than women, and to want sex more often than women do.
- Women want sex but they have been 'programmed' from way back to link sex with commitment because they needed their mate to stay around to protect them, especially if the result of sex was conception. Nowadays, even with contraception and with women being more open about enjoying sex for its own sake, there's still a prevailing value held by women against one night stands and for engaging in sex only after getting to know a man. In other words, depth of feeling (and therefore at least possible commitment) is properly associated with sex. This is fine and wise, but the point is that it contributes to many women's approach to sexual activity and readiness for arousal in a way that isn't quite the same for most men.
- Women are often unable to feel aroused when they don't feel loved and attended to. They want expressions of tenderness and closeness, which may not be forthcoming, in order to feel aroused sexually.
- Showing loving and romantic feelings is something men have suppressed, because controlled emotions are necessary for successful 'fighting' performance. Women think they need these things to feel aroused, and many men aren't good at showing them.
- Men want love and tend to be ready to show love through initiating sex. When they come home from outside activities away from their partners, feeling ready to give and take some love, they may feel ready for sex. Women tend to be ready for non-sexual kinds of communication expressions of love first. Herein lies a common, but nevertheless frequently misunderstood problem, which is often the source of tension resulting from both partners feeling misunderstood and rejected by each other.
- Because women have only just arrived at feeling free to be

sexually aware and active beings after generations of suppressed sexuality, there is still a lot of ignorance on the part of women about their bodies, how to pleasure their partner and how to pleasure themselves. Many women therefore have residual barriers to the enjoyment of sex. Naturally this inhibits the extent to which a woman may seek out sex. She isn't motivated to seek out and learn to enjoy something she hasn't been able to discover the full pleasures of.

- Men tend to have a number of misconceptions and frustrations about women. They often think that when women say they want to be shown more love, that flowers and gifts are what they need. They have difficulty accepting that daily stresses diminish her sexual readiness; that sex doesn't automatically make her feel good the way it does for them; that women often can't say what they really mean because they're confused about their sexuality; that they are 'too emotional'; that when they take steps to look attractive or show affection they aren't necessarily feeling aroused.
- Women have their own set of misconceptions and frustrations too. A woman often thinks that if a man loves her he'll want to be with her, really talk to her and be able to understand her; that men are often driven by immediate sexual desire which doesn't have much to do with real love; that if he loves her he'll know what to do to excite her and shouldn't need to be told; that if he loves her he'll share his deepest thoughts with her and automatically demonstrate his love in the ways she wants him to.
- Because we're more open about sex, and the pursuit of sexual satisfaction as a goal is so conspicuous in our popular culture, there is more pressure than ever to seek out satisfying sex; to be dissatisfied with less than frequent and excitingly varied sexual experiences. This influence on our expectations, along with other prominent media stereotypes of successful and therefore desirable males and females, places its own kind of extra pressure on what men and women think they should be getting. Another potentially destructive aspect of sexuality, to which we are all exposed from time to time through the mass media, is violent and incestuous sex, which is mainly associated with male sexual aggression. This can colour people's feelings about sexuality in decidedly negative ways.

Rather frequently, as a result of many of these unacknowledged facts and unchecked misconceptions, the following kind of problem develops. The woman often feels wanted only for sex which she resents, and the man feels unappreciated because he equates her enthusiasm for sex with her enthusiasm for him, and so feels unloved and withdraws. A complex mixture of guilt, ignorance, a desire to please and not to exert pressure, to make allowances for things like pregnancy, illness, fatigue, and a sense of obligation, causes him to not initiate sex as often as he'd like to, and causes her to engage in sex when she doesn't feel like it. This is a sure recipe for an unexciting and inadequate sex life! He says to himself 'What does she want, after all I do for her and the family?', and turns himself towards more reliable sources of affirmation by working harder, for example. In time, partly because of his more urgent drive for sex, he may contemplate an affair. She gets resentful with him for spending even more time away from her and hence from opportunities to show her the love she needs, and tends to assume she's unloveable because he doesn't spend enough time with her. She turns this resentment in on herself, blames herself and starts to devote more time to self-improvement, such as enhancing her image so she'll be more attractive to him, or getting involved in rewarding 'good works' and devoted parenting. But, substantially because of their gender differences in ability to communicate about emotional issues (especially sex which still is harder than most topics to discuss), sex doesn't get any better and the couple eventually give up and put the problem in the 'too hard basket'.

> We both thought we had a good relationship in every way until we reached a stumbling block about our sex-life. I was into being a mother to our two small children and working part-time. Dan was working in a new business which was the most demanding and time-consuming job he'd ever had. I felt I couldn't share my everyday stresses with him like I used to, because they seemed insignificant compared to his. Increasingly I found myself unable to feel keen about sex myself or interested in pleasuring him. I was battling fatigue and a sense of emotional isolation from him. He had neither the time or the energy to help around the house as much as he used to. His work burdens made him seem to need sex more while there was less time to come together emotionally, which I needed to do

to 'warm up' to feeling sexually interested. We used to joke about me getting some libido tablets to solve the problem! It wasn't that I couldn't enjoy sex ever or have orgasms, it was that I couldn't as often as he'd like me to, and he got fed up with us having 'quickies'. He'd get very churned up about me thinking he was sex-mad and feeling it was unreasonable to have to contain his natural drive to make love. It became quite a problem between us but luckily we never seemed to have a problem with talking about it freely, though doing something about it was a lot harder.

Solutions

If you have an uninteresting and inadequate sex life and your relationship is otherwise reasonably alright, then you will be able to do things to liven it up. *Like anything else in a relationship, sex won't just stay good or improve without you doing something about it.* Don't be tempted to think that when you move house she'll feel happier and more receptive or when you change jobs you'll be less preoccupied and be able to give her more attention. These day-to-day changes do affect your feelings about each other and how much affection you feel able to show, but aren't enough reason to leave the problem to take care of itself.

- Make the effort to put aside more time and privacy to talk together about what it is that you think you do with each other in the bedroom that you really like or don't like quite so much (because it doesn't do much for you or it turns you off). Include topics like what your fantasies and expectations are about sex. For example women wanting romantic seductions and men wanting to be masterful and dominant. Talk about how these stereotypes can set the scene for unhelpful assumptions about which of you should be taking the initiative, who should know automatically how to arouse and satisfy the other, and about being responsible for communicating to each other what you do and don't like.
- Accept that your partner is not responsible for your sexual pleasure. You are responsible for understanding your sexuality and communicating with your partner about it so you can stimulate and satisfy one another together.

- Introduce some variety, create some new atmospheres by adding interest to your usual setting.
- Get yourselves a couple of good manuals about sex and intimacy from the extensive range that is available (see Suggested reading). Use them first to check your knowledge about the facts of sex for men and women, and talk about what you find out. A common misunderstanding stems from ignorance about physiological differences in the nature of orgasm, and about the place of orgasm as the emphasis of all sexual activity.
- As soon as you both feel ready to, try some of the exercises in your manual together, making sure you follow the steps carefully. Share your responses to it frankly, and proceed at a pace that suits both of you. Creators of self-help sex programs have successfully assisted many couples using a method called 'sensate focus'. It systematically enhances partners' awareness of their own and each other's sensuality and pathways to arousal, as necessary training for more satisfying intercourse. You'll find sensate focus described in one of your books.
- Try to accept that relationships are constantly changing and that your sex life will also have its ups and downs.
- Above all, get into the habit of talking more than you have been about your sex life. The more you do this and acknowledge your reservations and hesitations, the safer you'll feel about talking more and more helpfully to each other.

If you or your partner have a specific sexual problem (such as painful intercourse, premature ejaculation, inability to reach orgasm, failure to sustain an erection etc.), self-help manuals can be useful. If they aren't, and you're sure you've followed the advice and instructions for these kinds of problems carefully, then you should consult a sexual counsellor or therapist.

If your relationship has deteriorated so that you feel you can't even approach the bedroom side of things it probably means you should attend to improving your everyday communication before you start on your sexual relationship. Try starting with some of the pointers in Chapter 4.

If you're unsure whether it's too late to revitalise your relationship, and sex is one of the disappointing aspects of it, here are some important questions you should ask yourselves concerning sex and gender. Thinking about them may help you understand what went wrong and whether you could do something about it.

Check list for men

- Have I blamed my partner's faults unfairly because I haven't taken into account and accepted her basic femaleness before trying to negotiate changes?
- Have I assumed that my partner isn't interested in sex, for the wrong reasons? Do I assume she doesn't like sex because she doesn't find me attractive and loveable, or is it that she doesn't need much sex? Have I misunderstood women and their sexuality?
- Have I avoided discussing our problems because I believed they were insoluble, when really it was because I feel uncomfortable and inadequate talking about emotional issues and can't stand it when she gets upset? Is this because deep-down I find it awkward dealing with intimate feelings?
- Do I accept that there is a need to talk about feelings and sex, or do I really think these things should take care of themselves?
- Do I resent my partner's independent life and tend to undermine it because I'm not comfortable with her accomplishments, and would rather have her more dependent on me?
- When she wants me to show her more love and affection, do I know what she really wants? Have I tried to help her tell me, and accept her position as valid in its own right?
- When she's upset about something, do I really try to help her explain her position in a way that takes into account her female ways of asserting herself, without using my tendency to dominate so I outstrip her in our discussions, and have my point of view prevail?

Check list for women

- Have I blamed my partner's faults unfairly because I don't take into account and accept his maleness before trying to negotiate changes?

- Have I assumed that he needs sex to satisfy his own needs and forgotten that sex is also an important way for him to show love?
- Have I really tried to talk to him about sex, or do I tend to expect him to know how to interest me without me telling him? Could this mean I'm making him responsible for my sexual enjoyment and interest?
- When I feel he doesn't show me enough love, do I tend to withdraw and resent him, or do I really try to tell him more about what it is I think I want?
- When we try to discuss something, do I tend to be confused about what I really think and not say what I mean in case he gets angry?
- Am I confused about what I really want out of marriage? Do I tend to blame my dissatisfaction on the relationship, when I should be learning more about what I want—independence, home-making or both—and asserting myself more instead of blaming him for not giving me a contented relationship?
- Am I in touch with my own sexuality? Is there more I could be doing to educate myself?

How you react to these kinds of questions will tell you what areas you need to work on if you decide to try and improve your present partnership. If the prospect of tackling the issues these questions raise makes you feel defeated or hopeless, then you've also learned something important about what could be possible.

4 Successful partnerships

While you're doubtful about your relationship and uncertain what to do, at some time you'll probably ask yourself what good relationships really have. You'll be trying to discover whether what you feel for your partner is love, and whether it's enough. The answers are very much an individual matter of course, because there's enormous variation in what people feel is a workable partnership and what they're prepared to contribute, accept and tolerate.

Perhaps you've accepted that the magic of the early relationship must change, but you're still undecided about whether what you've got will do for you. To help you answer this, we're going to look further at what qualities relationships that seem to work well have, and at the kinds of things you need to do to prevent a relationship getting stuck. We'll be presenting an overview of some of the basics of relationship improvement. This topic is of course at least a book or more in itself. The aim here is to help you consider whether your relationship could possibly be improved and how to get started at this, or to help you be surer about separating.

Some important facts about relationships

Consider the following points and ask yourself whether you have the qualities described:

- Healthy marriages are like good friendships. They are workable partnerships (not necessarily perfect ones) in which each person feels supported and respected by the other most of the time, and only sometimes disappointed or let down. Be realistic and not over-idealistic about what sort of relationship it's really possible to have!

- If you enjoy successful relationships you'll have an awareness and acceptance of yourself, your strengths and weaknesses, your impact on others, and the way others affect you. You can communicate accurately and genuinely about yourself to others, and they can therefore respond in ways that satisfy you.
- You each allow the other room to have their own opinions and feelings about things, and accept each other's position without necessarily agreeing with it or even always understanding it. Feelings can be discussed as easily as the weather!
- Each of you is an individual with your own thoughts, emotions, reactions, foibles, outside friendships etc. You can acknowledge your unique differences and interests without them being a threat or a challenge. If you have what it takes, you'll see your differences as a treasured part of your separateness. The relationship is what enables you both to develop yourselves fully.
- Each of you is responsible for your own feelings and reactions and you each accept this responsibility. Accurate communication ensures that you do this, and we'll demonstrate how this works with a 'Levelling' exercise later.
- All relationships, including healthy ones, have good and not-so-good periods. It's how well you manage the not-so-good periods that's crucial. In satisfying relationships, the ordinary ups and downs of life together are seen as part of the ongoing challenge of a partnership that's going places. The 'downs' are celebrated as opportunities to work on problems together.

These six points are the most important elements for successful relationships. If you look back at the Introduction under the heading 'What to aim for' you'll see that this list also contains many qualities essential to satisfying relationships.

Looking after your partnership

Successful relationships of course don't just happen, they are made. Here are some active steps you can take to nurture what you have together. Consider these even if you're sure it's too late. You will go on having relationships, or you may be able to start applying some of them to another relationship you've already started.

- Put some time into enjoying togetherness. You did this without thinking about it when you were first together, but now it takes effort to make sure this happens! Don't let this put you off. Make a list of at least six things you'd like to do together as a couple on your own. You're each different so don't expect the lists to be the same or to sympathise with each other's selection! Pick one from each of your lists to start with, and agree to make a time to do them both. Keep this up, and you'll find that putting time into your relationship (away from the children and other obligations) is strengthening and creates renewed closeness.
- Build into your family routine a definite structure which ensures you don't neglect talking. It's very easy to let things slip unless you have a fixed arrangement to do this. Take an hour a week, on a fixed night say, which is only altered by negotiation. Take turns at fixing an agenda. Some couples find coming together *every* evening at a fixed time to review the day—the good bits *and* the bad—works well. It's a time for sharing pleasant thoughts and experiences and affirming your feelings for one another. It doesn't mean having marital marathons all the time, you can always meet and agree to leave it for that day! But it ensures you're attending to the relationship and each other's feelings regularly.
- Everyone, especially someone close and dependent on you, wants to feel listened to. Never make a person feel you dismiss their point of view. You might think that you always listen, but check from time to time that however good your intentions are, your partner is really feeling they are able to put their point of view across and that you do listen. Never jump in too quickly with your reactions and alternative opinions.
- Make sure you work out some ground rules for approaching discussions, especially about topics you know to be sensitive. Your rules should include:
  - allowing provisional statements or opinions which may be subject to changes;

— agreeing that it's permissible to not know what you think about a particular issue;
— allowing topics addressed earlier to be reopened, and an approach or an opinion to be revised or added to;
— agreeing that you'll each listen and repeat back what you hear to check for misinterpretations and to seek clarification before making assumptions about apparent meanings and intentions (we'll look at a communication exercise called 'Mirroring' later);
— topics may not be discussed for more than a certain length of time at one sitting;
— neither partner may terminate without acknowledging they're doing this and the frame of mind they're doing it in. For example, if you must withdraw from the discussion by sulking, this event should be acknowledged and accepted.

All these rules are essential conditions for open and trusting communication.

- A favourite and controversial subject for differences of opinion between you is how to bring up the children. Remember, parenting is new to all of us first time around and continually presents new challenges which don't just take care of themselves. Make sure you discuss and formulate policies as a couple, if possible before they have to be put to use. Without reasonable solidarity between you about children, your relationship will be subject to extra pressures. But be realistic! Precisely because the two of you are different and are allowing free expression of your individuality, you won't always agree on the best line to take. Be willing to compromise occasionally and try an approach that isn't necessarily the one you have the best feeling about. Compromising is important to all issues in relationships of course, not just parenting matters.

Sometimes I'd come in on a 'discussion' between Anne and the children and be annoyed by hearing what seemed to be a clash of wills between our twelve-year old and Anne. I suppose I felt angry that it looked as if she had lost her proper parental hold over the children and was sparring with them as an equal. I would tend to want to react as an authoritative umpire, coming in with a firm decision on the issue which solved it at least on the surface. I think it's easier for fathers, who tend to be more distant from the children, to be more decisive with them. Anne found it humiliating to have me decide an issue she was having trouble convincing Jessica about. We had lots of discussions about this because we could both see it was affecting our relationship. Once we were able to work out how Anne felt, why I seemed to be able to come in with a policy without losing the children's regard for me (we think Anne was afraid of losing their love if she came over too strict with them), we were able to work out different ways of tackling the challenges of assertive near-teenagers! And a result was better teamwork as parents which had a very good effect on our relationship, and Anne felt less pressure with more support from me.

Here's an abbreviated list of these ways of caring for your relationship:

- Make time to do things together as a couple.
- Timetable regular talking opportunities.
- Cultivate the art of good listening.
- Establish rules for discussing sensitive topics.
- Prepare together in advance for extra challenges like parenting policies.

Preventive tension management

As well as looking after your relationship together, you can each actively do things yourselves about everyday tensions and frustrations you experience, to prevent them growing into problems between you.

1 If you're feeling cross or tense about something to do with the relationship, make a promise to yourself to do something about it. Don't just wait till it goes away and meanwhile take your feelings out on someone or something unrelated to the problem.
2 Communicate your feelings, including your negative ones, as honestly as you can, without being destructive. They can't be taken into account by your partner if they don't know about them. You'll find tension and anger build up in you because

you're not genuinely expressing what you feel, perhaps for fear of the consequences. You are more likely to be respected for communicating your point of view if you do it accurately.

> My wife Kate had a habit of interfering with my exchanges with the children in a way that always seemed to be critical of me. I'd be doing something with one of them, like showing them how to turn the oven on, and she'd come along and say something like 'What are you bothering to show that to Sally for? She doesn't want to learn to do that!'. In order not to have an argument or be critical of Kate in front of Sally, I'd say nothing and just quietly withdraw. I'd tend to say nothing for the sake of a quiet life when Kate would criticise me directly in front of the children, for something like doing the garden when she wanted the rubbish put out. What would happen was that I'd suppress my rage again and again, and then Kate would say something else undermining, and I'd explode and start getting angry and abusive all over the place. Then I'd be accused of using bad language and ranting and raving.
>
> Tension was building up inside me to boiling point. I had to do something about this, so I started to make a point of saying calmly at the time, before I withdrew, that I disagreed with her point of view and found a remark hurtful. This way everyone knew what I felt, but an argument was still avoided. And the tension didn't build up so much inside me. After a while Kate even stopped doing this quite so much. There's room for lots more improvement between us, but this was a good start and it seemed to mean the children stuck up for themselves a bit more instead of always aligning themselves with their assertive mother!

3 You may not be able to communicate your irritations and frustrations at precisely the moment you experience them, because all you're feeling is just tension and irritability. Try and identify *accurately* what it is that doesn't feel quite right or fair, and ask yourself whether your reaction is reasonable in the circumstances. For example, is it really his fault?, have I communicated my expectations to him?, can *I* change things so this doesn't happen? etc.

4 When you've identified what it really is that's upset or disappointed you and how it's made you feel, make an 'appointment' with your partner to discuss it, at a time when neither of

you is likely to be preoccupied with other things. Present your experience in a way that isn't accusing but is informative and helpful, and invite your partner's comments. Remember the ground rules for marital discussions outlined above, and remind yourselves of them if you need to.

5 Share your thoughts and ideas on the problem, decide on a plan of action if you can. Even if you can't, conclude your meeting with a summing up of where talking about it has got you (remember the rule on withdrawals above) and adjourn it for further consideration if it remains unresolved. Limit your meetings to half an hour.

The family setting

If you have children, your relationship isn't being conducted in isolation. You're not just a couple, you're the team at the head of a family. Your parenting responsibilities are a challenge to your relationship as well as being a source of enormous rewards for it. In a relationship that isn't working so well, parenting responsibilities can be the focus, like sex, of destructive influences on it, creating another downward spiral of dissatisfaction.

The spin-offs of a cared for, healthy relationship are far-reaching when it comes to children. As we saw in Chapter 1, children need a sense of security in order to develop the feeling of self-worth that is so necessary to healthy growth and the achievement of potential. Children get security from feeling loved, and from knowing that the people most important to them—Mum and Dad—feel good about each other, and can cooperate as parents. So if you're looking after your relationship you're giving your children great comfort and security, an ideal environment for them to thrive in. You're also providing your children with a very useful day-to-day demonstration of effective teamwork and problem-solving, as well as modelling mutual respect and cooperation between adults of both sexes. These are very useful lessons. And operating as a team means you will have established the basis for involving the children in family decision-making as they get older.

With both of you in touch with what each other's concerns and responsibilities are, your children will receive consistent input and you will not be open to their manipulation of you—something which happens when parents aren't sharing enough together about what's going on in the family. Alignments between one parent and the children, at the expense of the other parent's sense of involvement, are not good for either the parents as a couple or for the children.

Two heads are better than one for anything that's challenging and also demanding. With both of you communicating effectively, you'll each be able to take the occasional break for time-out from the children to recharge your parenting and partnering batteries, knowing that you're both in touch with each other's approaches and methods with the children. Time-out like this is good for your relationship.

More active caretaking

You may be curious about what more you can do for your relationship. You may want a bit more structure in what you do together, because you can't keep up the resolutions you've made. You may want to celebrate your relationship by enjoying new experiences together just to see where they take you. Here are three exercises as examples of relationship-enhancement techniques. You should find that trying these helps you decide about your present or alternative relationship, or whether you'd be likely to benefit from some professional counselling together. They're enjoyable once you get into them, and will certainly teach you something new about how you relate together.

Mirroring

Using a mirroring exercise is a popular way of helping a couple see how well (or how badly!) they may be communicating together. Most of us make assumptions about what other people actually say and mean a lot of the time. If you are experiencing conflict, then not saying what you really mean, not listening accurately, and not checking out your assumptions by repeating back what you think you've heard, is usually how arguments get started.

Follow these simple instructions carefully:

1 Set aside half an hour together, away from distractions.
2 Decide who will first be the 'sender', and who the 'receiver'.

3 The sender communicates a simple, neutral statement. For example 'I got really annoyed in the bank today, I feel like moving our account! The teller was so inefficient and unhelpful, I almost walked out.'
4 The receiver then paraphrases the sender's statement and asks for clarification, adding 'Is that what you meant?'
5 The sender then confirms that the receiver has understood *exactly*, or else clarifies their statement.
6 The receiver reparaphrases the statement, and checks their version with the sender, and again until the sender agrees that the receiver has got it exactly right as to content, feeling, intent, uncertainties etc.
7 Change roles and repeat the steps several times.

Take care not to burst in with what you think your partner might have meant, as distinct from what they actually said. You'll be tempted to do this. Remember that defining your partner's intentions for them is what gets you into communication difficulties. Watch this!

Levelling

This exercise is about *being responsible for your own feelings and communicating them accurately*. It helps you both avoid the dangers of having to guess (perhaps wrongly) about your partner's feelings. It also helps you learn not to blame your partner inappropriately or destructively. This causes them to be defensive of their position. It is very important in a relationship to be able to communicate openly without fear of being judged or your point of view being undermined. If your partner really listens, you will feel more confident about communicating accurately. Once again, make some uninterrupted time together and follow the steps carefully.

1 Think of something you think your partner does which annoys you. Tell them about it, but be sure to phrase it in the first person. Don't say 'You really upset me when you came home the other day with all that unnecessary extra shopping. You know we can't afford it, you're always spending.' Instead say 'When you came home with all that shopping, *I got really*

anxious because I'm worried about our budget and *I'm disappointed* and *angry* that you don't seem to be, and *I feel* you're always ignoring my concerns.'
2 Your partner's task is to just listen.
3 Then change roles and you be the listener.
4 Practise levelling together and gradually try to incorporate doing this into your everyday life as you get better at it.

To help you get your levelling statements right, make sure they always contain three parts. Every exchange between two people has three components—a setting, a particular message sent, and a particular reaction on the part of the receiver. *A person sends a message which is received in a certain way; they are not themselves responsible for the receiver's reaction.* With levelling your message should be a clear statement that says 'When I do or say this, in this situation, I act and feel this way.'

It's important if you're at all serious about improving your relationship, to practise levelling with positive statements too. Depending on the state of your relationship, you could do the exercise beginning with a positive one. It might go something like this: 'When we go out together like we did the other night, I really feel good when you take the trouble to pay me a compliment about my appearance, and I love it when you notice I've made an effort to look good.' Communicating responsibly and openly about grievances will clear the air. Remembering to do this about positive things too will make you feel more hopeful about the relationship.

You may find that trying to do communication exercises seems artificial and awkward at first. If you don't seem to be getting anywhere, don't give up till you've checked that you've really followed the steps accurately. Don't get too serious about them, and try and have a few laughs at yourselves together over them! Being able to be light-hearted, especially about important things, is a great diffuser of tension. It needn't trivialise the process.

Appreciating your relationship

When your relationship is frustrating you, it's very easy to focus all the time on what you don't like about it, and on your partner's apparent faults. A useful exercise for you to do on your own is to make an appraisal of what you think your relationship gives you that you value, in other words its positive side. Set aside some time to write a list of these things. The results will tell you more about what potential the relationship has. You could then suggest your partner does this exercise too, and you could share the results. You may find doing this helps you see things more clearly. Here's the sort of list you might come up with if your relationship is working well:

- We support each other unconditionally.
- We make decisions together mostly, and tend to respect the ones that we make separately.
- We allow each other separateness.
- We have values and attitudes in common which make decision-making pleasurable and non-competitive.
- We have good sex fairly often.
- We take pleasure in our children as individuals, and feel this pleasure as bonding to us as a couple.
- We communicate our moment-to-moment states of mind honestly without conveying a demand or expectation that the immediate needs underlying them must necessarily be met by the other.
- We allow each other to express our points of view about each other without creating obligations or defences.
- We communicate in our everyday words and actions a sense of mutual respect for our different points of view.
- We feel safe to express the full range of our emotionality.
- We facilitate one another's individual productivity, as well as our joint undertakings.

This list is the result of a person appraising their relationship to enhance her appreciation of it. She shared her list with her partner as an affirming exercise. All the points she came up with are characteristic of a healthy relationship. They do not however necessarily imply she couldn't make a list of things she didn't like about it. No relationship is all pluses! If you have major doubts about your marriage, you might also find it clarifying to similarly make a list of the things about it that you don't value. Things that you feel are restricting. You should then go through each item and ask yourself how much you can really blame the relationship for them.

Maintaining your relationship when it's troubled

You may be in the very common predicament of knowing there are problems, but finding your partner won't or can't seem to acknowledge this. Or you may be in the position of your partner having announced that they think they want to separate, but they don't want to discuss why. Nor do they wish to consider steps you might take together to try to improve things. (We look further at the consequences of these positions in Chapters 7 and 8.)

- Keep talking, even when you don't seem to be getting anywhere. It really is true that relationships fail because of communication breakdown. Talking, including expressing feelings and opinions quite heatedly, is always better than silent stand-offs. Talking often leads to more effective talking that takes the relationship somewhere different. Silence will never lead on to constructive talking, and is a stalemate. At best, it forces assumptions to be made by both of you (which are often way out) about where you're each at, assumptions which you have to use as the basis for decisions and actions, getting you into progressively deeper water because you don't or can't check them out.
- Get yourself a good book or two on looking after partnerships (see Suggested reading).
- Enlist your partner's willingness to go on a course or an occasion away together as a couple. A weekend away learning something new, with a private contract to use it as a chance to attend to each other in a special way you've agreed on, is a great way to put some new energy into your partnership.
- You may have a close friend and confidante with whom you can discuss your situation, so use this special resource and listen to their impressions. But remember that friends, because they want to be supportive and reinforcing, will tend to give you the sort of feedback they think you want to get. So they often agree with your point of view, rather than challenging it so as to stimulate potentially helpful new thoughts.
- Better still go and see a trained counsellor/therapist and talk about yourself, your life plan and what's happening in your key relationship. Although *your* current motive to do this probably stems from your relationship dilemmas, don't feel this step is

only for people seriously questioning the future of their relationship or having a personal crisis. Although it might seem a luxury, as a personal growth opportunity clarifying your priorities and your reactions to marriage with someone expert on generating new angles on your approach to life and people can be a great investment, and can equip you with some new insights to help you make useful changes, whatever eventually happens with your relationship.

Being responsible

You have to do active things to make changes happen in relationships. *Being pro-active about your life, acknowledging your own power to do and change things and putting this power into action, will get you the rewards you want and put you in charge of your circumstances.* Being reactive, letting your life happen merely by responding to people and events, will limit the rewards you get and make you feel powerless. In no area of your life does this principle apply more significantly than with your intimate relationships.

Regrettably, many of us don't realise the importance of actively caring for our relationship until it is troubled, and then we may find it very difficult to know what to do about it. Even when we know what we should be doing differently and more actively, we may find it difficult to sustain the discipline and application to make real and lasting changes. Many couples give up because they have made some effort and nothing seems to have changed. It is going to be hard, but the rewards are enormous. With real effort and good humour, relationship difficulties can be overcome. Avoiding a separation is an achievement to be proud of, and your enriched relationship will bring many satisfactions.

Separating, perhaps more especially after many years together and certainly when there are children, is always difficult and painful, not to mention profoundly disappointing. Nobody wants to have to accept a failure of such a far-reaching kind, to hurt the person they've spent a good part of their lives with, to permanently affect the lives of their children. No stone should be left unturned in the search for ways to improve or reorganise a relationship rather than abandon it. If you do separate, your life may be held back with guilt and regrets if you cannot look back satisfied that you acted responsibly—you did all you could to explore alternatives to separating.

If you're on the way towards separating and you haven't taken any real steps towards getting some help, you should. There is a vast array of helpful relationship-enrichment resources in the form of self-help programs, workshops, couples' groups, therapy-based courses, marriage guidance counselling, marital therapy etc. If you do decide you want to try and improve things, and your partner does too, you'll need to find an in-depth and comprehensive program that suits you, perhaps with the guidance of a counsellor or therapist, and perhaps beginning with some further reading (see Suggested reading). Unless your relationship troubles are fairly minor, you're both committed to participating in the process of making changes, and there aren't any great problems in other areas of your lives (which usually interact negatively with a relationship), then it's unlikely that you'll be able to find success just with self-help programs. You'll need the support, guidance and discipline that a professional helper can provide, to sustain your efforts and keep you on the right track. Don't be discouraged if you have a few false starts and disappointments. Making real changes in your life and in your relationships is a process of growth, and so you're bound to encounter some growing pains.

5 Children

It's not surprising that for many parents the children are the most important reason of all for making the right decision. Or that many parents in not very satisfying relationships don't separate because of them. Your feelings for your children, not to mention their's for you, will tug at your heartstrings in powerful ways over the question of separating. So an informed understanding of the likely effects of your decision on them is crucial for considering your options fully.

You'll also need to think about how you yourself are likely to adapt to the realities (both good and not-so-good) of the shared, perhaps part-time, parenting that's inevitable after a separation; and the complications of new parent figures in your children's lives.

If you've decided to separate, you'll need to know as much as possible about their position and their needs to adequately continue your responsibilities well into the future, from how to tell them to successfully managing co-parenting.

What we know about divorce and children

It used to be thought that children from so-called 'broken homes' were by definition off to a bad start in life, and were disadvantaged in various ways by their parents being divorced or separated. But as marriage breakdown became more common, providing an incentive for more systematic research to be done, this viewpoint changed. It became obvious that the extent to which children are affected by divorce depends on how much conflict they are exposed to during the marriage and after the separation. In some families a separation undoubtedly brings a welcome improvement in a child's family circumstances because it brings relief from conflict. So it isn't the fact of a divorce, but rather the family circumstances both before and after the separation that have the effect. It's continuing family conflict that is psychologically damaging to children, not the event of divorce itself. A reassuring, but not so very remarkable finding!

For years after a separation and right into adulthood, children go on wishing that their parents had stayed together. Even children who remember experiencing a lot of parental conflict at home say they would rather their parents hadn't split up. This is a reality, but think carefully before you conclude that you shouldn't split up. After all, there are probably lots of ways in which people grow up wishing things were different and having to make major adjustments to events which aren't ideal. We survive, and often we're even strengthened by the experience. And it doesn't mean that just because we wish our parents had stayed together we'd have necessarily been better off if they had, because we can't know how that would have worked out. What it does mean though, is that since your children would probably much rather you stuck together, you should try hard to improve your relationship. Children are a very good reason for working hard at making a marriage work, but they're not usually a good enough reason on their own for keeping an unsatisfactory marriage going, though you may decide to do this.

Researchers also have shown that the happiest children of divorce are those who are supported and sustained through the years after their parents' separation by being able to enjoy free-and-easy, continuous relationships with both their father *and* mother.

What this means is that if you can't get your marriage to work and you must separate, then *the successful cooperative parenting after divorce which is necessary for children to sustain their important relationships is the most valuable thing you can give your children to compensate for not having been able to go on living together*. This makes obvious sense, but again it's reassuring to know that the research supports it. And it's *good* news because though you may not be able to do anything about inflicting a divorce on your children, you *can* do a lot of things to make their adjustment to it relatively trouble-free. It also means that you should think carefully about opting out of their lives altogether in preference to having part-time or occasional contact with your children, an option some parents (especially fathers) feel they have to consider.

To sum up then, divorce itself isn't necessarily permanently damaging, but if you're not sensible, emotionally detached and flexible, you may be contributing to the fact that your child's post-divorce life is. *Actively encouraging a positive relationship between your children and your 'ex' is the best thing you can give them to make up for you being divorced.*

Getting to specifics

Children *are* affected emotionally in some way by their parents' separation, but usually only for a time of transition while everybody adjusts to the loss of the original family and gets used to new relationships. How they react to your separation and adjust to it over subsequent years will depend on three main things.

- How sensibly you yourselves handled the breakup and ongoing relationships, including those with new partners, and perhaps stepchildren too.
- Their age and stage of development at the time your separation became known to them.
- Their individual temperaments. For instance, whether they are the easygoing or anxious type by nature.

Children too young to understand what's going on commonly refuse to believe a separation is going to be permanent. Older children often bitterly resent it. Unless there are extreme circumstances of conflict, or perhaps abuse in the family, many children dream of their parents reconciling, sometimes going to considerable lengths to try and contrive this. Even constantly quarrelling parents are better than separated ones as far as the children are concerned, it seems. This reflects the profound longing children often experience for both their parents to be available to them all the time, and their sadness at the permanent separateness of their parents' two different worlds.

Children tend to take guilt on themselves about the separation. They are themselves the centre of their whole life and thinking, and therefore (so they feel) they must be the centre of their parents' world. So it follows that all their own minor and major misdemeanours must therefore have been what culminated in their parents deciding to break up the family. This is because younger children tend to experience their parents' imperfections as failings of their own. They can't afford to see those they are so dependent on as other than infallible.

Older children tend to be aligned with their same sex parent as a natural part of their identity development, and are often angry with their opposite-sex parent, who's the one they feel should have 'done better', who has failed and let them down.

Reassure yourself that most children are pretty resilient, sometimes surprisingly so. It takes a fair amount of sustained stress to disadvantage a child permanently. Some children are by nature slower than others in developing a sense of security and self-confidence. They may be the anxious, shy type, or the boisterous, assertive kind. Or they may be affected by a developmental handicap of some kind which affects their self-image, making them more vulnerable. Different temperamental characteristics may mean certain children cope better than others with the stress of family disruptions, and some may need more support and nurturing at difficult times. You may have or know of children who just seem to instinctively sail through life, others who seem to be worriers.

What to expect

- They'll probably be unable to understand or accept why it happened, and will feel angry about it as well as sad at various times.
- They'll probably not be able to talk about it to you much, so you'll have to guess what they're thinking. This doesn't mean they're not reacting to it in their own way. Confused and disturbing feelings are difficult to articulate.
- They'll hope for a long time that you'll get back together.
- They may show insecurity in various ways such as testing you out by resisting discipline, being clingy, or behaving babyishly.

- Teenagers will often be angry, and may behave in a detached, resigned way towards both of you. They may especially resent the idea of you taking up with new partners.

By being aware of things like the importance of self-esteem, a sense of security, love and freedom from conflict between loved caretakers, you can do an enormous amount to improve the quality of your child's life, and probably everybody else's too.

One or two further factors need taking into account, even with apparently resilient children. Only children may be more affected than others at separation time and in subsequent years. Care needs to be taken to ensure they are able to be the child they are, and are not made to feel too much of a companion to the parent they mostly live with. This can mean they are having to provide support to a parent at the expense of meeting their own emotional needs.

Siblings can be a great source of comfort to each other, through knowing that feelings of guilt are shared and being able to talk things over together as part of a group.

Children are very sensitive to the feelings their parents are radiating about everyone in the family, and it may surprise you just how much of what's going on that you're trying to hide they will in fact pick up. They mightn't be able to make sense of it, but they can certainly feel it, and the 'vibes' they get can inhibit their own freedom of feeling and guide their loyalties, especially in young children.

> It wasn't too bad after I'd got used to it, my Mum and Dad being separated. Dad still lives in our family house and Mum lives with her Mum, not too far away. So I go over to be with Mum from Tuesdays to Fridays usually. Mum says I can please myself, but Dad sometimes makes me feel I've been there too long and I should come home. I usually do anyway because he takes me sailing on Saturday mornings. I think I understand why they separated. They're very different. Mum's easygoing and more emotional. Dad's stricter and more organised and a bit serious. I'm glad I can spend time with both of them, but sometimes I wish they'd tell me what to do about when to be where. Then I wouldn't have to keep worrying about whether it's time I left Mum and went back to Dad's, or whether I should go over and see Mum for a few days. Sometimes when they

> say 'It's up to you, please yourself,' I wish they'd decide for me. I don't want to hurt either of their feelings and I think they notice how much time I spend where.

This twelve-year-old expressing his divided loyalties shows how parents, in an effort to keep the to and fro arrangements easygoing and flexible have, without realising it, placed their son in a position of having to worry about doing the right thing a lot of the time. This is a rather subtle sort of burden which can go unnoticed and one that a child can do without.

Continuing to be a parent

We've explained that enabling your children to go on having contact with you both is very important in their adjustment to your separation. Although co-parenting with an estranged partner isn't easy, it's enormously worthwhile for your children, providing you manage it well. Here are some of the reasons why:

- Contact with the parent who moved somewhere else helps children with thoughts like 'If I had behaved myself better, and not caused so many arguments between them, he wouldn't have gone. So it must be my fault. If he could hurt my feelings so much by going, he mustn't love me any more. I mustn't be good enough for him to stay so I must be bad.' As we noted earlier, it's not at all uncommon for children to blame themselves for their parents' separation, especially if they recall parental tensions being focused as they so often are on issues to do with them.
- Children can feel rejected and abandoned by the parent who moves elsewhere, however mutual the decision to separate is. Contact with the parent who 'leaves' helps reassure children that this bond is not altered, it just has to be reorganised, and protects against damage to their self-esteem and emerging identity.
- Children have a natural tendency to fill gaps in their knowledge and thinking with fantasy. Regular contact with a part-time parent enables them to sustain a concept of that parent based on reality, rather than what they want to believe, or feel

pressured to believe because of the attitudes and feelings being communicated about this parent by the other.

- Young children who feel they have 'lost' a parent because they went away, can become worried about the remaining parent leaving too. This can mean that their sense of security is threatened to the extent that they are more likely to themselves incorporate the views, attitudes and feelings of their major caretaker, sometimes at the expense of their relationship with their part-time parent. Being able to see both of you easily helps restore a sense of security about the family, and enables them to have relationships that are more balanced and independent.
- Today's shared parenting, with both fathers and mothers (and often other caretakers too) contributing substantially, has shown that children can have important bonds with several people from a very early age. A child can really pine for a relationship lost through separation, even though the love of their long-standing major caretaker remains constant.

Thinking about future parenting arrangements

For most parents, the practicalities of who is going to live where, are governed by things like caretaking patterns to date, employment factors, access to adequate accommodation, finances, the children's ages and personalities etc. Often considering these factors helps make decisions about arrangements, at least in the short-term, a fairly obvious choice. The principles which should guide your decisions about who lives where are discussed further in Chapter 8 along with other decisions which follow on from separating. Whatever the arrangements, they must, as we've seen, allow you both to continue to be actively part of your children's lives, even though one of you may be spending less time with them from now on. Try and start the arrangements for both having time with them as soon as possible after you separate, to demonstrate to the children that family life and having good times together really are going to continue.

In deciding where you're both going to live, bear in mind that although you might feel you want distance from your partner to enable you to get on with your own life, the regularity, frequency and flexibility of your children's contact with both of you will be made easier if you're not too far apart. But be assured that if this can't be, it is possible for a child to conduct a meaningful relationship and sustain an important bond with a distant parent over time, even if you can't spend as much time as you'd both like together.

Once you have a plan for everyone's living arrangements your next task is to tell the children you're separating.

Breaking the news

How you do this is very important, and you'll probably be quite worried about it. Caught up as you'll both be in your own emotions about separating means it's easy to do this ineffectively or even to avoid it altogether. If you tell them nothing at all they may invent their own reasons, perhaps inaccurate or even disturbing ones, for why you're splitting up. Talking with them gives them the reassurance they need so their sense of their own worth is not damaged by the experience of a major disruption to family life. Keeping them informed will help them feel involved in what's happening to their family, and will combat the inevitable sense of insecurity about the future.

Discuss it between yourselves first. From now on, despite your adult differences, everything that concerns the children should continue to be your joint responsibility. They need to feel you are still a team for them, if not for each other. This can begin with sharing the responsibility of telling the children what's going to happen. So try to do this together after you've prepared yourselves as a couple.

> We agonised for many months about whether we should tell the children, what we should say, and when would be the best moment. Despite our many differences, we both had in common a very sincere concern for our three children. While there was still a possibility that we might be able to save our marriage, there didn't seem to be any point in unsettling them. Our oldest child was preparing for important exams so we thought it best to leave it till he'd finished them. At one time I didn't feel I could talk to them about us

> separating without telling them that it was their Dad who was breaking up the family not me. And he didn't want to announce it at all if I was going to make him out the baddie, causing them to take sides. Then we tried to agree on whether it was best to tell them while we were still living together so they could take in the idea while we were still both around to talk to about it. Or whether in fact it wouldn't really mean anything to them if we didn't put the separation into effect straightaway.
>
> I'm glad in a way that we kept putting it off because when we did do it we were both more composed about it ourselves, and could present a more united and reassuring front.

It's best if you can tell the children something before you actually do separate, so that it has time to sink in, so questions can be asked and reassurances given, while you're both around and accessible. The content of your explanation will depend very much on the children's ages and your separation circumstances. Here are some guidelines:

- Acknowledge the importance of the event by saying that it's been a very difficult decision, one not taken lightly, and one that will be hard, in different ways, for everyone in the family to get used to.
- Try to convey your reasons for separating in a simple way with just enough detail to satisfy their curiosity and make them feel they can ask questions of both of you when they want to. A fairly general statement about liking each other in some ways, but being unable to live together any more because you're too different on too many issues, will often be sufficient, especially if they've seen you in conflict.
- Try to use language that explains things in a non-threatening way without actually covering up the truth too much. You can say that Dad or Mum is going away, but this doesn't mean they don't care for you anymore; that they care for each other still, but in a different way. That means they can't live together anymore; that family life will go on but in a new way from now on, which will take some getting used to, but will be a bit of an adventure in some ways, with plenty of opportunities for them to spend time with both Mum and Dad.
- Leave out the bits which cast doubt on the integrity of a parent,

like frequent infidelities, alcoholic rages, irresponsible expenditure, deceits, frank disrespect for one another etc. Try to sound as if you support and respect one another's view so that the children sense you can be a team. This sounds obvious but despite everything, you may find you're doing and saying things on the spur of the moment that aren't very teamlike.

- Say that some of the things that go wrong between parents are difficult to explain, and you know it mightn't be very easy to understand why it has to happen, but that they should try not to worry too much about reasons, or about which of you might be most at fault.
- They don't have to know the truth about who's to blame or who did what in the past, even though you may find you very much want them to know and accept your version of events. Much of what happens in adult relationships is far too complex for children to really understand anyway, and you may confuse and distress them. If you think that you really do want your children to know 'the facts', stop yourself and consider what the effects of insisting on the record being set straight will be to their feelings. More about this in the section on helpful attitudes.
- A useful approach with older children is to describe what's happened in terms of marriage and adult love relationships in general. This dilutes the failings of you in particular as parents, and makes some statements about families which may be valuable to them later on. Older children can, if you pitch it right, learn some important things about adults and about relationships from what you say to them, as well as come to respect the way their parents dealt with the breakup.
- Younger children tend to be rather black and white in their thinking. For example, if they think Dad has left for a new relationship, then he must be wicked through and through. Both of you need to help your children understand that their parents have many strengths, and these aren't cancelled out by perceived faults.
- Say that both good things and sad things will come from the changes, and that everyone will feel a bit unsettled while they adjust to the new arrangements.
- Reassure them of your absolutely unchanged love for them, of

the fact that they'll still see both of you often. Explain your arrangements for this.
- Give lots of reassurances whenever you can, that what's happened between you is quite definitely not their fault.
- Don't expect them to react immediately. It'll take a while for it all to sink in. Make sure they feel they can talk more about it with either of you when they're ready to.

If you can't do the telling together, because you've already split up and weren't able to prepare the children before, or you know it's going to be unpleasantly emotional if you try to, at least agree on roughly what you're each going to say to them, and when you're going to do it. The reality may be that your partner has already left before you really realised the relationship was that bad. Then it's much harder to explain things, because you don't really know what's happened or what's to come, and feel hurt and angry. You must still try to reassure them that family life will continue, expressing yourself in a way that preserves their feelings about their other parent, whatever you might be feeling about them. Bear in mind the points above and adapt them to fit your circumstances. Even if you're burning with rage, hurt and sadness, you must try to convey your reasons for having to separate as if you both contributed to the difficulties. You probably did, though you mightn't see it this way right now.

If you know that you're pretty hurt and angry about it all, be extra careful that what you say to the children doesn't place all the blame on your partner. Try to remember how much harder it'll be for the children to go on loving both of you if one is portrayed as having done great wrong to the other. It's often extremely difficult to do this if you're very resentful and didn't want to separate, but it's very important to do whatever you can to prevent your children taking sides. If you don't know what's going to happen about their contact with your partner, it's a bit harder. Try to reassure them anyway, without making any firm promises that may end up in disappointments.

During the difficult period when everybody's adjusting to a different kind of family life, be especially careful not to do or say anything which could undermine their love for a parent or confuse them. Their relationship with whichever one of you 'left' can be especially fragile to begin with. They may be feeling abandoned, sad and angry.

Taking an honest look at the realities of post-divorce parenting

Here's what's going to be asked of you if you're to get shared parenting reasonably right for your children. You need to know what you're going to be in for so you can decide if you're up to it.

Being a parent after a separation isn't that different to being a parent in a marriage. The children go on needing you to be involved, enthusiastic, reliable and consistent. It helps to think of the extra complications and frustrations of limited communication as challenges rather than problems. Early on you'll feel a bit inadequate as a parent. This is a natural result of having to accept you've failed as a partner, of having to adjust to the new pressures of being on your own, and having to resolve your ongoing feelings about your partner. For a period of about twelve months many parents say their parenting suffered.

Don't spend too much time worrying about how the children are faring. There's a danger that looking out for problems (a result of guilt and anxiety) creates problems that aren't really there. A certain amount of worry of course is useful because it keeps you watchful. But it's pointless worrying more than a little. You can't change the fact of your divorce so it makes far more sense to make the best of it, helping your children get some useful experience in managing life's hurdles through your support and guidance.

Spending less time with the children now than you did or would like to is a tough one. You may feel ill at ease on your own with the children to begin with. You may miss them terribly. Perhaps you feel out of touch with them now that a good deal of their daily lives has nothing to do with you. Maybe you feel you can have no lasting effect on their progress and development. Many of the things you sense about their separate lives with your ex-partner are not what you'd really like for them. They're growing up in ways you don't readily identify with, and would like to change but can't. Most part-time parents must face these sorts of realities. Many of these matter more to them than they really do in the long run to their children. But however determined you are to put their needs first, these potential frustrations are very real. On the positive side, you may find that regularly spending time on your own with them, free from the relationship stresses, makes for more relaxed, resourceful and enjoyable times together than you've had before.

Helpful attitudes for co-parenting

Here are some guidelines which will show you some possible danger zones for the future, and how to steer through them. You should expect issues that can become problems to crop up from time to time even if you've separated months or even years ago. If you're a parent, prepare yourself for life after separation by thinking about these points in advance.

- Realise that there's always more than one point of view to things. For any relationship to work, each person must allow the other room to have their own opinions and feelings, and respect each other's position without necessarily agreeing with it. As we've noted already, this is a key factor for successful relationships. It applies no less to your separated relationship. Never make a person feel you dismiss their point of view. Everyone wants to feel they're listened to. You might think that you always do listen, but check from time to time that however good your intentions are, your estranged partner really feels you do. You'll find all your differences of opinion with your former partner harder to deal with now because they're no longer able to be balanced out with love like they were in the good old days. The differences are now all centred on the children, for whom your love and concern hasn't changed. Remember, they have two parents who are different people with different strengths and weaknesses, both of whom in their own individual ways are important sources of learning for them. When you get exasperated, try to see it this way, and always be prepared not only to listen, but also to compromise.
- Recognise that it's difficult to have real solidarity as a couple when you don't see or talk to each other much. But this is what children need in a family. Aim to work as a team for your

children. It *is* possible to be reasonably united about them on minimum communication, especially if you can be detached enough from issues of fairness, deservingness and blame, to see that making compromises rather than pressing a point just for the sake of it, is often worthwhile. Check yourself regularly about why you want to insist on something going your way.

- If you've started a new partnership, it's even more important than before to have couple solidarity in this relationship. You have the extra challenges of step-relations this time. You can't effectively manage all the complex relationships and meet everyone's changing needs without the authority of united leadership. Make sure you set aside time to talk over family policies and practices regularly as a couple and include time to trustingly share your feelings about everyone (the good ones as well as the bad ones!). You'll find more about this in Chapter 9.
- When you feel needy, a bit hard done by, or just lonely, do a double check on yourself to make sure you aren't drawing more emotional support from your children than is really good for them. Being a parent after a separation can be more lonely than you expected, and you'll feel inadequate at times. Remember, the children need you to be involved, enthusiastic, reliable and consistent. At times this will seem a tall order. It isn't good for them to see you as down and fragile to the extent that they have to worry about you, perhaps feeling they have to provide you with sympathy, support and companionship. They should be getting these from you, not providing them for you. Obviously you can't always cover up or deny your feelings. You need to try and be real and human rather than controlled and edgy so the children feel able to open up to you when they want to, but don't feel they have to worry too much about how you are. You can acknowledge some of your feelings to them if you take care to do it in a way that doesn't make you seem frail as a parent, as if *you* need *them*. They need to see you strong and positive about the future, so their own sense of security about it is preserved.
- If you find yourself preoccupied with who did what and said what in the past, and who believes whose version of events, you may be anxious that the children see you as you think they should. It's hard when they ask questions about the past, and you must answer in a supportive not blame-placing way. You

may be tempted to involve them in your adult emotional business because you're worried about what they may be thinking about you. Or you may be concerned about the influence of their other parent on their thoughts about these grown-up matters. It's harder still if you feel anxious about how their relationship with a step-parent (your 'ex's' new partner) is going to develop. It's natural to fear being 'replaced' by an alternative same-sex parent. If you do get into a detailed discussion about family events and personalities you may place children in a conflict of loyalties that can be emotionally difficult for them. Realise that separated parents are often worried about how much influence they will respectively have on their children as time goes on. Understandably they may have doubts about how useful a parent they will really be able to be on limited time together. Try to believe in yourself and what you can offer your child without feeling the need to prove it to them by setting the record straight or asserting your biological superiority over a step-parent.

- There's often something else at work within this uncertainty about the strength of your bonds with your child. It's an aspect of the loyalty triangle which children have to come to grips with. They want and need to go on loving two people who don't love each other. Since you no longer love your child's other parent, and aren't part of their relationship with this person any more, there is a subtle sense in which you parents may have become rivals for your child's affections. They may seem in your mind to have a choice now about where to place their loyalties, a choice they didn't have in the same way before, when you all lived together. You may find yourself worrying about how much time they want to to spend with you; whether it's more fun for them at Dad's place; is their bond with Mum growing stronger at the expense of their ties and loyalties towards you? If you are feeling lonely, isolated from your family, or you haven't really got your life reorganised adequately yet, these sorts of doubts may affect the way you relate to your child. Then you're not giving them the freedom they should have to adjust to and enjoy their new relationships freely. It'll be affected by various obligations, demands and pressures experienced because of where they sense you're at. You're leaning on them a bit too much yourself because of your own needs and a new sense of competing parental influences. You need to acquire the strength not to be threatened by or jealous of your child having strong emotional links with someone who is now outside your family circle, a relationship which you can't be any part of. This can take some adjusting to and requires a sense of personal security that is sometimes shaken after a separation.

- Never lose sight of the fact that your child is entitled to enjoy the freedom to relate to both their parents (and step-parents too) in their own way, at their own pace. They have to take in and make some sort of sense of the various features, both similar and different, of both of you (and of your present partners, if you have them, and their children). You can't expect to be able to influence how your child reacts to their other parent or to a step-parent, how many of their characteristics and standards they choose to model, internalise or ignore. Every parent passes a milestone when they help their child progress confidently from the early period when they are completely dependent on you and directly share all of their waking experiences with you, to allowing them to have separate experiences you are not at all part of. It can be much harder to give this freedom when your child is spending impressionable time with someone you have emotional feeling for, whether this person is your child's natural parent or a step-parent.
- A young child's quite natural needs for security may be such that they will show what seems to be indifference or criticism of one parent so as to please the other. It's not hard to see then how Mum for instance, could get quite the wrong idea about her child's feelings about their father and therefore their contact with him, when what she's seeing in her children stems from their relationship with her, not with their father at all.

We never liked going back to Mum's after a weekend with Dad. We always had a good time, what with no school and Dad making a fuss of us. When we were home, Mum always made us feel we shouldn't be too enthusiastic about Dad, and if we said anything she'd ask more and we'd feel a bit like we were getting the third degree. Sometimes I even said something not very nice about Dad's girlfriend just for the sake of it. And on Saturday mornings we really looked forward to seeing Dad, but we didn't like to seem too keen to leave Mum behind us, so we didn't show it.

This story shows how children in a touching effort to please both their parents, gave their mother the impression they weren't that enthusiastic about their time with Dad. She might, especially if she was still carrying negative feelings herself about him and had doubts about her own parenting, start to think that they weren't having a good time with him. Children should be able to relate to both their parents without having to devise elaborate coping strategies to protect their relationships in this sort of way.

Children are quite materialistic, especially during the period from about age eight to their teenage years. If you are able to provide a lot of material attractions you may create a longing in a child for your sort of life in the belief that being with you is somehow better because of what you offer. This longing can also develop because life in one household seems to be more free and easy, or leisure-focused, than in the other, because it happens at weekends and holidays. These differences don't matter in themselves, but letting a child feel they have a choice about their arrangements if they express their preferences is mistaken, because they have to be preferences about one parent at the expense of the other.

Knowing when to act and what to do

At some time or another you may ask yourself whether what you observe in your child's behaviour is something you should be doing more about than you already are. More, that is, than being confident, cheery, low-key, reassuring, positive and patient.

As we've said, it's unlikely that your child will react to your being divorced in a seriously pathological way, so don't be too ready later on, after you've separated, to attribute what you see of concern in your child to his family circumstances. And don't spend too much time blaming yourself and the fact that your marriage didn't work. This isn't fruitful.

Most children will show some signs that they are feeling troubled by what's happening in their family. You need to know that things like clinging insecurity, silent withdrawal, anger manifested in aggression or tantrums, sadness, lack of self-confidence, deterioration in school performance, distractibility, unsettling dreams and sleep disturbances are all part of children's reactions to stress and change, and as such are ways of coping. You may notice that your child seems to have reverted back to a stage of competence that you thought they had progressed beyond, like not wanting to leave your side or wetting their bed at night. Almost all children show some kind of unexpected behaviour from time to time as they develop and mature. Usually it doesn't last for long, so don't be alarmed or feel guilty. Neither of these reactions will help. Blaming it on something you think your partner should be doing differently won't help much either unless you can talk things over really trustingly with them.

After considering this, if you think there's cause for concern about your child and how they're coping with life, first discuss your observations with your current partner and confidante, your 'ex', your child's teacher, and see what your combined thoughts can do to shed light on whether you have a problem that you could all assist with. If this doesn't work then consider seeking expert help. A good counsellor may be able to help you talk more constructively with your 'ex', if you're having trouble doing this. Problems that seem as if they are something to do with separation events are usually best dealt with by consultation and discussion between parents and a counsellor rather than (and certainly before) singling the child out as individually having a problem requiring treatment. But if your child's social, family or school life seems severely impaired over a considerable period of time, then consider consulting a child-guidance professional. Keeping a record of all that you have observed of concern will help them to help you with the problem.

Don't forget that the power to help make your child's life more comfortable lies with you, because of the close relationship you have together, and because you can help them with self-expression about their world, encouraging open communication about it.

Talking about family matters after separation

Having navigated the tricky business of telling the children that you're separating, it won't be long before you realise this is just the beginning of your new parenting responsibilities. Hopefully you've achieved this first step in such a way that the children feel the topic of family and changes can be opened up at any time in the future. What you say to children over the years has a great bearing on how they perceive the reasons for why things are the way they are. So it's worth addressing further how to manage topics like fault, truth and feelings.

When the family is reorganised and the children know that both of you are still available to them but on a new basis, they may want to ask questions from time to time, often quite out of the blue. You may find yourself uncertain about how to answer them the best way. It's important that they feel they can refer to what happened between you, that it's not a taboo subject because they sense you're reluctant to discuss it. They may decide that what you aren't telling them must be something really awful if it has to be secret. Keep your answers to their questions simple but sufficient to satisfy their curiosity. Try to lead their enquiries on, without being too pressing. Keep it fairly low-key, using their question to give some supportive information and explanations.

> It's hard to strike a happy medium about how much to reveal especially when they ask you questions like 'Is it true Dad that you haven't given us any money for three weeks?' You have to resist the temptation to answer with the absolute truth and try to say something which isn't quite a lie, but which takes the burden of worrying about adult differences away from them. I think I said something about how family finances had to be rearranged and we were still working things out, that seeing things differently was one of the reasons we couldn't go on living together. In fact I was furious because I'd been sending her the agreed amounts regularly, and it enraged me to think she must be involving the children in a hard-luck story at the expense of my reputation with them. But if I'd given them the facts, it would have put them in the position of wondering which of their loved parents was the biggest liar! It's hard getting control of your own feelings in time to do the right thing by the kids.

Don't forget there are certain things children can't be expected to understand because they are very adult or complex. Such as the idea of romantic love—that not loving someone anymore doesn't mean you hate them. Don't be tempted to volunteer too much detail in explanations or announcements. Young children especially cannot begin to understand the affairs of adults, and you will risk making them confused and anxious if you try too hard to have them know what happened.

At all costs try to keep communication channels open between you and your children. It can help them accept and even begin to understand their own feelings if they are able to express them to someone they trust. Not just feelings about divorce matters either, about everything. Many parents are afraid to talk about emotional issues, sensitive or not, and find it hard to do this in a calm and instructive way.

Children need parents to be able to give them emotional guidance and advice about feelings and relationships just as much as they need this about the educational, social and recreational parts of their lives. It's a great mistake to neglect this, but a rather frequent one. They should be allowed and encouraged to express their thoughts and feelings within the family. Then you can help them acknowledge, understand and contain their confused emotions and sometimes unnecessary anxieties in helpful and healthy ways.

But don't feel you must make a huge thing of talking about it often, or worrying about their feelings all the time. Your separation is a fact which you've all got to face, and which can't be changed. It's best dealt with, after the initial announcement and discussion, with good cheer, brave hearts, acknowledgment of mixed feelings and a positive outlook.

If both of you can continue to relate to your children in an open way which is respectful of each of your contributions to the family, past and present, then communication will be more likely to remain open and productive all round. This will mean that everyone's adjustment to the new and changing circumstances is going to be much, much easier. And children will be readier to take on the challenges of being part of two households and of forming new relationships within them.

To summarise the main issues concerning children, here's another check list of questions to ask yourself. Your answers will help you work out how prepared you are to separate.

- How skillful and patient will I be able to be about my partner's reactions to us separating? (How I handle this is going to affect my children's adjustment to it.)

- Can I put the necessary effort into being a parent on my own, supporting my partner's such efforts?
- How do I feel about my 'ex' having someone new in their life, and the effect of this on my children and their relationship with me?
- If we stay together because I don't want to inflict a separation on the children, what sort of relationship will we be able to have? Will it allow the children to progress satisfactorily, even if I remain dissatisfied with my marriage?
- Have I informed myself adequately about the likely effects of us separating on the children? Am I being too alarmist or too optimistic?
- Have I got what it takes to put aside my feelings about my partner for the sake of my children's wellbeing?
- Have we worked out a sensible plan for how and what to tell the children?

6 Triangles

The single most important fact about alternative relationships, affairs, lovers—whatever you choose to name them—is that when a partnership has become a triangle, you think and feel differently about it in very significant ways. The experience or prospect of another relationship has a profound bearing on what options you're willing to contemplate and what decisions you end up making about your longstanding one. You may not realise this, but it's true. You may know that an affair happened because you weren't happy, but you probably won't be aware of how much this event is affecting how you feel about your personal life.

The message of this book remember, is about the importance of making decisions from an informed rather than a reactive standpoint. So it's not a matter of implying that you shouldn't be getting into another relationship, although it always makes things more complicated. This is a matter for you. But you should know what having someone else does to you and your partner's feelings, and your respective vision about both the present and the future. So common is it for separations to involve a third person and so profoundly does it affect you both (whether you admit it or not) that this chapter is devoted to equipping you with better insight about what goes on in triangles, linking in the themes of earlier chapters as they apply.

What affairs do

For someone facing the prospect of separating, the question on the face of it seems to be either 'Is what I might develop with this person going to be better than what I've got?' or 'Can our relationship survive this event and continue in spite of it?', or 'How can I convince him that I was unhappy for years, I'm not just leaving to be with someone else?' Underneath these obvious and necessary questions lies a more fundamental one. This is how the presence of this person in your lives is governing your feelings about the past and the future, clouding your vision about what could be possible in your marriage, closing off options that might otherwise seem more available emotionally, sending you in a direction you might otherwise not so readily be going. This is the really important question to be addressing, and the one which is often ignored and certainly difficult to answer. But unless you apply yourselves to answering it, you're likely to cut off some possibly worthwhile options without fully realising this is happening. The apparent sanctuary of a new relationship, or deep resentment about a partner's infidelity, will tend to disguise what's really going on so that the dissatisfactions in your primary relationship remain unresolved.

For many couples, the first real crisis in their relationship comes when an affair is discovered. A relationship can be unattended for years but it's when most people's greatest fear, that there's someone else, that separation may first really be considered.

Affairs almost always mean there's something wrong with the primary relationship. The other relationship is the symptom of the underlying problem, and is not itself the cause of it. It doesn't matter how serious or even how sexual the other relationship is for the person who's got into it, it's how much it threatens the betrayed partner and hence the relationship that counts. A second important fact follows from this, which is that however much either of you can acknowledge that your relationship has had its problems, an affair often causes emotional reactions that precipitate the end, removing for one or both of you the possibility of staying together.

An affair's power to devastate a relationship exists for most Western-minded partners. Sexual intimacy is a very binding part of marriage and long-term love relationships. Whatever your moral and spiritual standpoint is about sex and affairs, however open-minded you might think you are about it, for most of us sex is what separates a permanent love relationship from other kinds of companionship. We define our primary relationships as sexually and emotionally committed, so that if we find sexual and emotional interest outside of one, we are taking away the very thing that makes it exclusive, diluting our commitment to it. We have opened up the possibility of finding elsewhere what we thought was, and should be, what made our primary relationship special. This is bound to affect it, usually in a damaging way, at least for a time. For one there is a withdrawal of commitment, along with guilt, secrecy and a new kind of indecision. For the other, once it's discovered, there is a new kind of threat to a relationship hitherto assumed to be secure, and a sense therefore of trust having been betrayed. No wonder affairs are such powerful marriage-breakers.

You have three main options when faced with a problem in your relationship, however the problem is manifesting itself. To take charge and make a commitment to try and resolve the problems and stay together, to do nothing, or to separate. Keep calm and try, despite your hurt or your guilt, to see it as a message that you both need to do something constructive about. Accept your feelings about being in a triangle as normal and reasonable, but don't do anything too decisive immediately while your feelings are running high. As usual, before you make any decisions with long-term consequences, take a look at some facts, acquire some information.

Why do affairs happen?

They happen because many people think the solution to an unsatisfactory relationship is to change partners. They try this solution out 'on the side' to see if it works. They have needs that aren't being met in the marriage, perhaps because of boredom or estrangement, but they aren't ready or willing to go as far as separating. They haven't got the self-confidence to get out of a bad relationship any way other than by attaching themselves to someone else. They believe an ability to experience an exciting new relationship tells them that their old relationship can't be made to work.

There are also people who have an attraction to novelty and an apparent disdain for real commitment, who seem to need the gratification that attracting partners gives them, as if they're 'hooked' on easy love. They feel insecure about their acceptability and attractiveness to people and reassure themselves through new and exciting relationships. They have deep-seated fears about the real intimacy of committed partnerships. There are others who feel angry about their marriage and have an affair as a form of protest. They look elsewhere because their partner won't give them what they want. Or they feel frustrated with their marriage or their partner's apparent refusal to acknowledge their dissatisfaction, and don't know what to do about it. They try and see if they can find what they want with someone else without leaving their marriage, or before seriously considering doing so.

Still others find themselves, as if by chance, letting another relationship begin when up to that point they thought they were perfectly happy. They didn't know they seriously lacked anything and the affair served to tell them so. This often happens when you're unable to express your feelings very well. You deny they exist and turn from your marriage to an affair to express affection and sexuality.

When affairs remain secret, it may seem to be because of a desire to protect the wronged partner's feelings, to avoid taking full responsibility for either relationship, to avoid causing hurt when the marriage might improve or the affair might end. It may be because you value your established partnership highly, even though sex of the quality you find in other relationships doesn't seem available in it any more. Keeping your secret is in fact a way of doing nothing about the reasons for needing two relationships, and also of course a way of avoiding facing your primary partner's reactions.

The feelings of betrayal when you discover an affair has been going on for months or years are extremely damaging. You may be able to cope better with the sexual side of the infidelity than you can with the emotional bonding that goes with it because this feels like the greatest threat to your relationship. Finding out that a significant relationship has been going on without your knowledge is usually the most difficult part to adjust to, because trust is destroyed. Discovering you have been living for a period while something important has been going on you didn't know about is almost more damaging than the fact itself.

The partner having the affair has their own strong emotions too. There is guilt over the deception, attraction to one person at the expense of their feelings for another (some of which may still be strong), and resulting massive uncertainty about what to do which may go on for some time.

So there are all sorts of reasons, some more subtle than others, why new relationships get started, and you'll begin to see further as we go into what underlies some of them, why it's such a common occurrence. Most of them are bound up with our dependency needs, the mysterious attractions of romantic forces, and in gender differences in emotional expression. So we'll look at all of these factors.

Dependency in triangles

We've seen how dependency and love get mixed up, so that it's hard to know how much of your feelings for a person are real love or are more to do with your need to feel real through living for another. A dependent person may deny what's not working well in their relationship, naming their partner's affair as the problem because they need to hang on to the relationship with all their partner's faults. They could not survive without their cause, their reason for living. This person may forgive an affair so as to sustain the relationship, but will never address and resolve their own emotions about it. We noted that dependent people are good at denying their own feelings because they define their lives through other people's needs and feelings.

Such a person's partner may feel driven to an affair which feels more emotionally sustaining than their marriage. A partner who is dependent on their relationship to give their lives meaning and to achieve a sense of wholeness is often someone who cannot give their partner what they need emotionally. Their partner may well be attracted by the apparent comfort and ready support of an alternative relationship, though their own dependency may prevent them actually leaving their established one. We've seen how early on in a relationship, we tend to deny our real selves in the interests of giving lovingly and that after the initial bonding, our separate selves must re-emerge for the relationship to sustain productively for both people. You may attribute a potential to this new untested relationship because it makes you feel more readily satisfied now. You think you've found a way to meet some of your needs better than you seem to be able to in your marriage. This relatively new relationship may well be unable to go on giving you these feelings once it has faced the test of time and the necessary re-emergence of two separate selves.

Another dependent person may be so hungry for emotional sustenance, feel so undervalued in their neglected relationship that an affair feels like something really important and powerful because it seems to give them these things. They contemplate changing partners to get what they need because they haven't learned how to meet their needs themselves. They are once again acting as if they can find happiness from and through another person. The feelings are so powerful that they read them as a sign that their present partner is the wrong one, using their relationship to govern their decision-making, and never addressing why it was that they couldn't get what they wanted from their established partner. They will carry their misunderstood dependency into the new relationship.

When you think about these two examples of how dependency and limited selfhood can operate, it's not hard to see how you can be influenced by your relationships to make decisions which may not be informed ones, and indeed why second marriages often don't fare much better than first ones. If you rely only on the quality of a relationship to make you feel whole, alive, powerful and optimistic, then you will be very tempted by the attractions of an alternative relationship as a reason to move on. You will also be very vulnerable to being abandoned by your partner's decision to leave, taking a long time to recover and likely to submerge yourself in another relationship as soon as you can. A reminder: everyone is dependent to some degree, and everyone uses other people to guide their decisions in life. *When you are guided entirely by your needs for other people you won't know that you may be making decisions which aren't the best for you. Or you may get stuck believing the restoration of a much-needed relationship will solve your problems.* Then your dependency is working against your finding lasting satisfaction in relationships.

Misunderstood dependency may make affairs very seductive, causing you to believe another relationship will solve your problems, when it hasn't even been tested. It may make you unable to see an affair as other than a character defect on the part of your partner, blinding you to your contribution to the relationship's problems. You desperately want the relationship back so you'll forgive the 'misconduct' as long as it isn't repeated, or even go on tolerating your partner's affairs. Your new relationship may help you feel stronger about leaving your existing one. You may discover that you don't need it as much as you thought you did, once you've separated. It gave you a sense of strength, wholeness and power to do something about your marriage.

I had another relationship going while I was still with my husband for quite a while before we eventually separated. I'd been dissatisfied for years really, and what I had with Brian made me realise what a relationship could really be like, and helped me to know I must separate. Brian made me feel alive and strong. Strong enough I suppose to get on with trying to negotiate an amicable separation, something I'd been putting off. Anthony (my husband) knew about Brian, and although he said if our relationship was finished then I was entitled to keep company with whoever I wanted to, he was very angry and I don't think he really felt okay about it until he found someone else. He refused to allow Brian near the house even after he'd gone, or to let him have anything to do with the children who weren't so young anymore and, I thought, quite able to handle my having someone else. He was so angry about Brian that at one stage he wanted to try and get legal custody of the children. I knew it was a punishing thing because his plans didn't leave room for day-to-day management of them, and they'd have had to change schools. His concerns for them all seemed to be focused on Brian's supposed bad influence on them.

Strangely enough, although I thought Brian and I would go from strength to strength once my separation was sorted out, we haven't been seeing that much of each other lately. He had left his wife not long before we got together and there was a lot of unfinished family business left over from that relationship that was starting to catch up with us. I'm enjoying being separated and I can see that whatever might happen between Brian and myself in the future, having him in my life served the purpose of making me feel sure enough and confident enough to end a worn-out marriage and gave me support through it all. But I can see that Brian's involvement made it a lot harder for Anthony and that we might have had a less traumatic separation without him in my life. On the other hand, I might still be with Anthony doing nothing about my marriage.

Romantic attraction and new relationships

Many affairs happen at, or soon after, the time comes to negotiate the transition from the period of romantic love into a satisfying long-term relationship. We discussed the many myths associated with romantic love in Chapter 2. Most of them have a great bearing on affairs and what we decide to do about them.

If you react to the changes in your primary relationship over time as if you believe the excitement of its beginning will automatically continue and that if it doesn't then there's something wrong with it, you'll be tempted to look elsewhere for romantic feelings. You'll probably find them. Then you'll face several problems. The contrast between what you find outside your marriage and what you have at home will be sharp. Remind yourself of the dynamics of new love that make you feel all-powerful, instantly giving and receiving warmth and pleasure and finding a sense of oneness with a person. Remember how the excitement of these sensations can blind you to the real qualities of your newfound love. Beware making major decisions on the basis of these intense feelings until you've fully considered how they might be affecting your perspective. You'll be tempted to think that your new relationship does have qualities you don't have in your marriage and that therefore it's got a better chance. It may do, but you are comparing an exciting new and untested relationship with what your marriage seems to be like after time and neglect.

This is an unfair comparison. You're putting side by side a relationship that has weathered years of family life, in which longstanding habits and familiarity have developed, with a relatively new one which is constrained by your marital status, perhaps intensified by secrecy and by unexplored and uncertain prospects. You probably haven't even reached the stage of having to make the necessary transition to a long-term commitment with your new partner. And yet it seems so delightful. How are you going to weigh up these strong feelings with your sense of history about your long-term partner and your love for your children which will be undermined by your leaving them? How will you know when to tell your partner, whether to suspend the affair while you try to improve your marriage? How will you deal with the guilt about your partner's reactions? You're in for a disturbing time deciding what to do.

You cannot know what a relationship's potential is—whatever condition it's in—while you are conducting more than one. If you decide to leave your partner to pursue the new relationship because it seems to have a sparkle that your marriage has lost, fine. You may discover that you find some excitement that lasts longer, but be aware that at the time you made this decision you didn't know whether either of the two relationships could give you long-term satisfaction. If you decide to go on dealing with your boredom at home by seeking romantic excitement elsewhere, nothing much is going to change. You won't find out whether either kind of relationship could lead to greater satisfaction.

If you suspect or discover that your partner has someone else, remind yourself after the doubts or the shock, of how attractive new love can be. Remember how yours used to feel? Think about what you both might have contributed because of your expectations about romantic love to what's tempted your partner. You both have contributed to all that has happened in your relationship. Use this truth about relationships to help you with feeling that you've been replaced because you weren't good enough to keep your partner faithful, because it's not all your fault. It's not all your partner's either. Perhaps you have neglected your marriage because you've been assuming exciting, continually romantic relationships just happen. A neglected relationship is a vulnerable one. To wait (even unconsciously) till there's a crisis like a rival relationship before you take more active steps about yours, means you're caught up in the myth about romantic relationships just happening of their own accord. This enables you to blame the crisis on your partner's actions. Their way of responding to what they aren't getting with you may be reprehensible and deeply hurtful, but hopefully you've by now discovered that it's almost always mistaken to see relationship breakdowns as one partner's fault. It certainly isn't helpful to you in the long run.

Sex and alternative relationships

The many reasons why affairs happen tend to be different for men and for women. One is sex and it shouldn't be too surprising from what was said in Chapter 3 how the scene gets set for alternative sexual relationships to be attractive, however much we might want to have better sex with our partners, and however guilty and secretive we feel about the way we've dealt with the problem. Men tend to be more easily tempted into affairs for primarily sexual motives than women are. If their marriage is a few years old and 'that old magic' has worn off a bit, the fresh excitement of a new liaison with effortless sexual highs may make a man think this new relationship is justified.

The 'other woman' is responsive because of the newness and sometimes the exciting illicitness of the relationship. Her receptiveness makes him feel loved and therefore more able to show the love she needs to enjoy satisfying sex. It's not that more men than women leave marriages—in fact the reverse tends to be true—but that one of the reasons men leave for other women is partly, and perhaps significantly, a sexual one. Many people think that good sex happens just because of a good relationship, and that finding better sex means this relationship is a better one. And men, because they are good at denying certain feelings, tend to avoid facing relationship problems because this involves acknowledging difficult feelings. They tend to act on relationship disappointment by exploring new possibilities.

Women are more able to express their dissatisfaction in relationships and make the first move to try and resolve them, but often find their man unable to discuss them. They are more likely to leave relationships to have a period of time on their own, to 'sort themselves out' before getting involved again, though often their needs—just like men's for love and sex—cause them to enter a new relationship sooner than they'd planned to. Both men and women often nominate feeling undervalued by their partner as the problem in their relationship, and find themselves ready to enter another relationship because it makes them feel eligible, reassuringly affirmed and youthful. These are important and seductive feelings which may seem to have gone from their marriage. Women tend to be especially attracted to a new relationship to get a much-needed sense of worth and instant affection. While they may not be driven so immediately by sexual needs, they may look to another relationship because it makes them feel able to change and move forwards out of a marriage which wasn't working but which they depended upon, like Anthony's wife above. At the same time they may discover they are suddenly more able to enjoy good sex. Remember the fact that novelty makes for instant sexual excitement, and inclines you to forget that sustaining sexual satisfaction over time takes effort.

Given that most of us value long-term relationships and good sex (both goals we had in our marriage), then added to these complex motives has to be the right kind of opportunity for another relationship to get started. Most people say the friendship 'just happened', they didn't go out looking for it. For example, many men have plenty of opportunities to meet women they may be attracted to through their work activities and time spent outside the home. Available women, perhaps younger and unattached, and therefore attractive, are there. Women who are involved primarily in home-based activities may have less opportunity to meet possible partners and less readily available 'cover' than their partners.

Does it mean the end?

We know that in working relationships couples can tackle problems and issues effectively. Job changes, parenthood, bereavement, illness and other more minor everyday stresses are tackled jointly, and solutions are generated that are mutually satisfactory. Finding yourself having an affair may tell you perhaps for the first time that you're seriously questioning your marriage, and that it's time to really get down to talking about what can be done. Your partner may not be able to see it this way. They are more likely to see it as a character defect on your part, at least initially. This is a major barrier to the possibility of rediscovering the trust necessary to weather the event and find a new kind of relationship together.

Try to see the existence of the other relationship and your feelings as a hurdle you may be able to overcome, although it's the biggest and most emotional one you'll probably ever face. An affair and its discovery can often serve the useful purpose of forcing you both to address your relationship. Although there's no denying the real hurt and anguish that the event causes, couples do adjust to affairs and continue together in a better kind of relationship. You'll need to be able to work through, perhaps with the help of marital counselling, the guilty and angry reactions, and the profound feelings of hurt and inadequacy the 'wronged' partner usually has. To do this successfully the 'wronged' partner, often the woman, must learn to establish a new kind of trust in her partner.

> We had been separated for a year and a half, but still met from time to time and discussed whether we could get back together. I wanted to, and Tom said he also did but wasn't sure what he wanted, or whether we could be happy. He had had an affair which came out in the open just before we separated. I said I forgave him, and this was a real surprise to him. Perhaps it would have been easier for him if I hadn't, so that my position on it could have been what finished our relationship for good. But I found that even a long time later I was frightened it could happen again, and frightened of my extreme distress about the affair which would still come to the surface sometimes. I realised that unless we could really resolve the event together, there was no future. He didn't seem to be able or willing to examine it, he'd say he wasn't good at discussing deep issues and didn't see the need to. So we had a stalemate for a long time which prevented either of us getting on with new relationships or making a commitment to working at restoring ours.

For the relationship to survive an affair both of you must acknowledge joint responsibility for the relationship problems that gave rise to it, as well as the 'guilty party's' responsibility for acting on the problems in this way. Only if this is possible can the relationship begin on a new basis, and the real issues of how to make it more mutually affirming and sexually rewarding be addressed. Understanding and acknowledging your different gender needs and dependencies is an important part of this process. It may prove impossible to save the damaged relationship if the 'wronged' person is unable to resolve their feelings of hurt and inadequacy, or if their partner isn't willing to suspend the affair to address the issues in a committed way. Then the relationship must end.

The trouble with affairs is that they tend to make working at a marriage often seem harder than leaving it, causing you to think repairing it is impossible so you avoid making a real effort. It's as if, were it not for having the option of another relationship, we would be more inclined to work harder at this one. If another relationship feels better than an existing one, and you aren't willing to suspend your new one while you thoroughly examine the possibilities for the established one, then be aware that you haven't really answered the question: Could we have made it work? Accept also that your new partner is no guarantee for a successful relationship. You haven't discovered what your contribution to how your longstanding relationship ended up, and so it's likely that you will bring your characteristic ways of handling relationships—the good, the bad, and the unknown ones—into your next one.

If you're going to try and work on your existing relationship, and do this properly so you arrive at an answer about its future, it's going to need your full attention and commitment. You'll find it hard to give this unless you suspend potentially rival relationships. Even if you think you can keep another one on hold for three months or so while you try, it may be harder to convince your partner that you really did try, with your other relationship in the background.

> Looking back on our attempts at restarting our marriage on a new footing, I don't think we ever got past first base. I felt sincerely willing to do whatever was necessary to save it. We got a bit stuck with trying to communicate what was wrong with the relationship. She'd say what I want is a really meaningful partnership and I don't feel I have that with you. I'd say, what is it that you're not getting now, maybe I can make some changes. She'd reply by saying that I couldn't really love her or I'd know what she meant and I'd understand her. This was terribly frustrating because it meant we couldn't get on with doing anything together. She insisted that the problems in our relationship were longstanding. The biggest problem for me is that she formed a relationship which (although she's reluctant to say much about it in respect for my feelings) I know she thinks made her feel understood and gave her a depth of feeling which contrasted strongly with what she feels we've ever had between us. I'm convinced we'd have got much further together if he hadn't been in the emotional background, even though she said she'd ended the relationship.

Restoring trust

An affair is bound to mean a loss of faith in the relationship. If the relationship is to survive the crisis of an affair, it must be redefined on a new basis and the relationship as it used to be left behind. After all, once the assumption of fidelity has been shattered, the relationship never will be quite the same again, and both of you in your different ways will be uncertain as to whether the situation could repeat itself. We all believe that trust is essential to a workable relationship, and to a certain extent this is true. But we need to re-examine what we really mean by trust, what we want from a partner who has betrayed it, what we are willing to do to earn back our partner's faith in us and in the relationship when something's happened to damage it.

To restore trust in the relationship, the person who has damaged it must do some things to earn it back. If you are able to be frank and honest about the rival relationship and your reasons for having it, then your partner is less likely to stay suspicious. If you are prepared to try and make the relationship work despite your fears that you may be let down again, then you're giving your partner the opportunity to show that your renewed trust in them, and in a new kind of relationship, was well founded. Both these requirements for re-establishing trust involve an element of risk. Whether taking these risks proves worthwhile will require time and frank exchanges.

Meanwhile you both need to ask yourselves whether what you thought you meant by trust is in fact realistic. Many people think trust means knowing someone so well that they can always predict how they will behave, that they always know and understand their innermost thoughts and moods, that their partner is there for life. People are individuals with separate selves and changing feelings, which cannot be reliably predicted by anyone else. *The only person you can really know, predict and completely rely on for inner security is yourself.* If your assumption of trust means all your security is tied up in this relationship, perhaps you are confusing trust with blind faith. This is an unrealistic expectation which doesn't allow the separateness necessary for a lasting relationship with another.

The kind of trust necessary for a satisfying and lasting relationship is really more about respect and tolerance than complete trust. It involves acknowledging that both of you have the power to damage the other's confidence in the relationship at any given time, because you have separate selves. It involves being committed enough to doing things for the relationship because you want rather than have to be in it, and because you want to earn and enjoy respect and tolerance.

Timing

It would be easy to say it's more sensible not to get into another relationship because it only confuses things and makes decisions harder to make. But not many people conduct their emotional lives very sensibly. Emotions, especially those concerned with love, aren't very amenable to forward planning or strategic timing for most of us. We all have needs and drives which we want to express. We have profound uncertainties about relationships which means we need to use the existence of alternative ones for comparisons to guide our decision-making and to reassure ourselves about our future prospects on the eligibility stakes.

If you're contemplating another relationship, and in that sense have some choice about whether to take it further now, it's worth considering some of the key points we've already made before you proceed. Comparing a new and limited kind of relationship with an established one may blind you to the potential left in the latter. It's also true that many people who leave one relationship and go straight into exploring the possibilities of another one (however cautiously!) tend to find as we saw in Chapter 2 that they get into the same kinds of difficulties (though they may recognise them earlier this time) as they did in their previous one. If you believe an unsatisfactory relationship is best resolved by acquiring a new partner then you're really acting as if you think your problems were due to your partner's failings. This is almost always a myth. Yes, you may indeed find something that's better with someone new, but your best chance of it lasting is if you take active steps to apply to it what you've learnt about yourself from the relationship you've left behind.

A period of time on your own before you make a full commitment to a new relationship will help you sort out things like how enticed you can be to a relatively exciting new romance when you're still faced with decisions about the apparent hopelessness of the existing one. It will help to discover how much your own normal dependency is making you inclined to cling to relationships and be blinded to their real qualities, and how much your maleness or femaleness is governing what you want from and do in relationships. We all know this at a rational level, but we all also have needs which we want to meet and which only can be met in relationships. We may have fears that someone we've found who gives us the hope of a new start mightn't be prepared to wait around while we sort ourselves and the existing relationship out. Many people's sense of worth is such that they have little confidence about finding a new partner in the future, and feel that they must respond when opportunity knocks. These are all powerful influences on your decision-making.

Once you've considered this chapter, try taking another look at the checklists in Chapters 1, 2 and 3. Referring back to these questions and the issues they raise will help you work out what to do about your position as part of a triangle.

7 The turning point

Relationship problems manifest themselves in as many different ways as there are different kinds of people. Some couples argue overtly a lot of the time, never really solving the issues they're fighting about. They get good at patching things up for the time being because life has to go on. For other couples there are never any apparent arguments as such, but the relationship continues with issues never being brought up for fear of confrontation, or because one or other isn't in touch with what they really think and feel about their marriage and can't therefore express their views. They get good at leaving things unexpressed because life has to go on. For other couples the outward problem centres around a known habit ranging from something like one partner spending too much time at work or at the pub, having affairs or gambling, to an alcohol problem or physical violence. The perceived problem serves as the ongoing focus for the relationship problem as if, were this corrected, the marriage would be alright.

However they show themselves, once there are problems a process has begun which will progress towards a gradually mounting sense of frustration in the relationship, or at best a manageable but limited kind of partnership without real closeness.

Deteriorating relationships

The symptoms of relationship breakdown only tell us what's happening on the surface. They don't tell us why we become so dissatisfied with the partner we so lovingly selected to begin with.

Or why we get stuck in a pattern of progressively unproductive ways of relating, blaming our partner for having changed (he's not the person I married), or for having disguised their true character (she didn't show me how submissive she was when we first met). We've seen that the way people function in relationships stems from the misunderstood dynamics of romantic love, dependency and gender expectations. And that these dynamics carry over unhelpfully into troubled relationships and interfere with a couple's ability to constructively address their problems. We'll take another look here at how our need to depend on another gets mixed up with romantic feelings and contributes to how things often go wrong.

Paradoxically, the very qualities that so endeared you to your partner in the beginning are often those which in time start to irritate. Swept away by positive feelings, we couldn't anticipate the long-term side effects of our loved one's masterful dominance that so attracted us, which now makes us feel over-directed or unable to have a point of view. We may be irritated by what seems to be a submissive dependency which stems from what we once saw as attractive femininity. We enjoyed the thrill of finding someone we felt complemented us, had traits which rounded us off as people so we seemed like a balanced team. As two whole separate people (not one!) we each have varying needs to sometimes be more dominant and more dependent which have to emerge with time just because we *are* two separate beings. So when we find that our partner isn't the person they seemed at first, isn't like we'd like them to be, we feel disappointed and we protest at their apparent changes. We experience great underlying anxiety when we find our needs aren't always being met. We feel angry about our partner's perceived deficiencies which sets in train the familiar characteristic of blaming the relationship's problems on their partner that troubled couples have.

Recalling our earlier exploration of the links between how we were parented and how we handle adult love relationships in Chapter 2, *it is as if we've arrived at the same point in our marriage as we were at when we first realised our parents weren't infallible and we had to stop expecting them to be. This is a major turning point in a relationship. How you deal with the discovery that your partner can't give you all you want determines the future of your relationship.*

Here's an outline of the stages characteristic of relationships that don't go anywhere very satisfying from this point on. First, we are shocked at the dawning reality that our partner isn't quite what we thought we'd married. We feel so disappointed that we then try to deny the reality of having discovered that we aren't going to automatically live happily ever after by making allowances, minimising our partner's negative qualities, hoping they'll go away. But reality catches up with us, and the full discomfort of the difference between what we thought we'd found and what we've got makes us feel betrayed by the emergence of our partner's true qualities. This is when some couples part.

Others, having acknowledged that their dissatisfaction is real, then go into a bargaining stage where they try to improve things by making deals such as 'If you helped me more round the house, gave up going to the pub, I'd become more interested in sex'. This sometimes appears to help for a while, but the underlying problem of you each wanting the other to be different often doesn't ever get acknowledged, and the undertakings aren't usually kept up for long.

The last stage of a failing relationship is when you give up any hope of finding what you want in it, and you either separate, or carry on in a sort of parallel living arrangement sustained by increased activities centred outside the relationship or by commitment to parenting, keeping up the outward appearance of a marriage.

Emotions and facing the issues

Most of us in fact just stumble along through these stages not really knowing what we're doing or what's happening. As the fact of having relationship problems that must be faced emerges, we become anxious and our anxiety further prevents us being rational and objective. *We cannot take charge and start doing constructive things about the problems because anxiety interferes, causing us to be reactive and defensive*. We defend ourselves against expected hurt, usually by withdrawing, and our ability to express ourselves clearly and assertively is inhibited.

A common way of dealing with anxiety is by getting angry. Anger makes us ready to attack with competing accusations, to dominate our partner by bringing them round to see things our way, placing the blame for the relationship problems outside ourselves. This makes us unable to come together to discuss problems in a balanced way, so that more arguments and stand offs follow. We assume that the problem is the other's fault (they've changed or begun to show their true colours). Attempts at discussing problems in the context of extreme anxiety, frustration and anger, combined with this mistaken belief that the relationship can be fixed by the other changing in ways defined by you, are major barriers to resolving problems.

When feelings are intense you tend to react (defend, challenge, disagree, compete etc.) instead of listening, observing and thinking. We also focus almost exclusively on our partner as we see and experience them, at the expense of looking at ourselves. This results in our being unable to see or even contemplate any other point of view on an issue other than our own, which prevents us finding new ways of managing the relationship. We approach attempts at solving problems together by reacting in ways which give short-term relief and reassurance but don't get us any closer to our partners in the longer term.

The ways we react to anxiety are habitual and reflex and are difficult to change, especially while a relationship is troubled. Our feelings override our intellect and our rationality so we can't think about ourselves or the relationship with much objectivity at all. The real underlying problem doesn't get addressed, that is, *why* you're angry and anxious, and *why* you're blaming all the problems on your partner. When we react with anger and disappointment we are less able to tell our partners what we really want. If they ask us we often react by saying things like 'If you really loved me you'd know what I want'. Rather than telling them clearly we tend to withdraw our affection and create emotional distance, enlarging the gulf between us.

Relationships often get stuck here, with both people feeling frustrated. Attempts to fix things only seem to lead to more confrontations or stalemates.

Making changes

As we've seen, many people react to their relationship difficulties with thoughts like 'If only they'd be different or pull their socks up, we'd be happy'. When we point our finger at our partner's perceived faults, wishing they'd be different to feel okay ourselves and save the marriage, we're behaving as if we thought that our partner were responsible for meeting our needs. *A relationship cannot be truly improved for long by each partner making a list of the things they'd like the other to fix up.* Contracts like this only help if you're also working on communicating better and enhancing the positive side of the relationship, and thinking about what your own needs for your partner to be different really reflect about you. On their own, they emphasise individual faults and tend to foster a competitive spirit about who's doing the most to fix up their deficiencies. They don't get to the root of the problem. They reinforce the misguided idea that a relationship can be made to work by each partner defining what sort of person they'd like the other to be, which means changing them into someone they aren't! No one's dissatisfactions are ever truly solved by living someone else's life for them (defining how they should be), or by seeking self-definition from another (becoming the sort of person your partner seems to want). This is why making deals won't usually work, and the changes you each undertake to make don't happen or don't last, as so many couples complain.

It doesn't mean that partnerships don't involve give and take, compromise, concessions and changes. It's just that for a relationship to grow and improve the process of making changes has to be different. It must start with permitting a person to be what they are, *accepting responsibility yourself for getting your needs met, and for your feelings and reactions to your partner.* Communicating openly and trustingly together about each other's needs and feelings is the only basis for making lasting changes. When you've listened uncritically to your partner and reflected on how you can contribute to meeting their needs as well as your own, you'll know about how the ways you behave affect your partner and therefore be more able to understand the real reasons behind their reactions to them. This cooperative and accepting way of making changes in the interests of the partnership is quite different from trade-offs like agreeing to get home from the office earlier (when you'd rather be working late) because she's accusing you of neglecting her, in exchange for her keeping the house more shipshape for you (when she's quite happy with the way she runs it).

Changes which help the relationship will work if they're made because you want to make them, rather than because your partner has identified a fault in you or is threatening to leave. You will want to make them if you're attending together to talking, exchanging and closeness at the same time.

We talked about the importance of separateness (as well as connectedness) in healthy relationships in Chapter I and elsewhere. To recap, the single most important realisation you have to make to achieve a lasting relationship with another, is that your partner is an individual with needs and feelings that are not, and cannot, be governed by how much they might suit you. The moment you can say *'I accept all the bits of my partner which mightn't please me, and I can see them as part of their essential character, and I am responsible myself for my reactions to them'*, you'll stop trying to change them and be well on the way to being able to make the relationship work.

Why facing problems takes time

There are two things most relationship breakdowns have in common, whatever the outward symptoms are. They take place over time and they proceed at different paces for each of the partners. Both these facts have an important bearing on separation events.

Nobody wants their marriage to be a failure so we're reluctant to face the real issues for many months, even years before they build up to the point where they are inescapable. Factors like children and other commitments, fear of the future, employment fortunes, and low self-confidence interact with the relationship issues to extend the time before which the real problems have to be faced and then acted upon. This is understandable when you've made a commitment about which doubts are surfacing and adjustments are having to be made. Our reluctance to face the uncomfortable reality of being unhappy in our marriage causes us to avoid clear signs of real problems and we just soldier on trying to be forgiving, understanding and accepting, looking elsewhere in our lives for sources of satisfaction and positive feelings when things don't seem to be able to change.

Apart from none of us wanting to really take in what's going on that isn't so good, this gradual pace is also because, while we might be facing doubts in our head, we're wary of talking about them. We want to be sure about them. We want to avoid hurting our partner by expressing new feelings. We aren't very good at expressing ourselves intimately anyway. When we know something is going to be hard or awkward we tend to bury our heads in the sand and hope the feelings will go away of their own accord (remember our tendency to think relationships just happen?). We feel a sense of failure and consequent guilt, blaming ourselves for being dissatisfied, for wanting to question a sincere commitment we made. We're frightened about what our doubts will do to our partner, uncertain whether we should be expecting more. A period of time which may last months or even years is needed, to come to terms with doubts and questions within ourselves. In this time there are often periods of relative calm and apparent easing of the problems, which makes us inclined to think they've gone away and can be left alone.

Letting things progress to this stage means that it's hard to break out of the habitual rut of just coping, and move into a better kind of more open, aware and freedom-permitting relationship. By the time you both begin to acknowledge the fact that there are problems, it often happens that one of you has lost faith in the relationship and has become detached and resigned. Many more marriages would be able to be revitalised if people were more aware of the consequences of not attending to their relationships from the beginning, acknowledging what's really happening in them and acting upon it before it becomes too late.

So separating is a gradual process, and however much one partner might think of the final parting as the moment of breakdown, in reality things have been happening more or less consciously for both partners for a long time before an eventual parting.

Becoming aware that there are problems runs at a different pace for each person. This fact further extends the time it takes to address what's going on. There are two sets of expectations about what makes an adequate relationship, two sets of dependencies preventing balanced communication and creating varying fears of the future, different needs to hang on to or leave the relationship. Men are often less able to acknowledge difficulties because they tend to deny uncomfortable feelings. It's true that in a marriage one partner can be genuinely dissatisfied at the same time that the other thinks they're quite happy. But it's the fact that these two positions can't be allowed or discussed that's the problem rather than the difference between the two positions itself.

It's the way the 'downs' in a relationship are tackled that is always the stumbling block, particularly the 'down' of not being able to discuss your doubts or your confidences about its future together. The pattern of dealing with the downs tends to be set long before the question becomes 'What's happening in our relationship? I'm worried.' If the prerequisites for effective communication (see Chapter 4) aren't there or cannot be learned then when the subject of the relationship has to come up, either competitive arguments or frustrated silent stand offs occur. In both cases assumptions are made about each other's point of view because they aren't listening to each other. Both ways of dealing with the sensitive issues of relationships are stalemates, because nothing gets interpreted or expressed accurately and nothing gets resolved.

Many couples manage this state of affairs for many years, by making the most of the good things that the relationship provides, devoting themselves to parenting and career activities, getting on with activities outside the marriage with more energy. This is a way of expressing a hope that the problems will go away. It's a form of compromise that works for some people, or it may serve as a bridging period of transition before an eventual separation further down the track.

You may be having doubts and wanting to do something about it, knowing how important it is to get talking together, but finding your partner unreceptive. They appear unable to recognise the reality that you are experiencing, and aren't ready or willing to address the relationship with you. This is a very common difficulty and it tends to mean that you progress further and further towards separating as time goes on because you can't address what's going on together. A man is often dissatisfied about a relationship but can't communicate this effectively, leaving his partner unaware of his concerns. A woman may be dissatisfied and wanting to talk, but is unable to get her partner talking with her. You two individuals are therefore proceeding at different paces towards acknowledging the problems and perhaps facing up to possibly separating. The partner who's unwilling to acknowledge the problems is denying there are any, misleading their partner. The one who knows there are problems but cannot enlist their partner's acknowledgement of them becomes ever more frustrated.

> I had been feeling dissatisfied for a long time and I tried to get David to talk with me about what was happening. I think he felt that I was going to blame him for what was happening between us and insist he made some changes. Whenever I tried to talk to him it was never a good time, there was always something else he had to do, or he'd make me feel I was imagining things and didn't have a valid point of view. Eventually I said to him I wanted us to go for marriage counselling and he said that was only for people with real problems and that he wouldn't come with me. I got so frustrated that I went to see someone on my own which helped a bit. But what I really wanted was to work on the issues together, rather than have to make a decision on my own about whether to stay in the marriage. It wasn't until I went to see a lawyer about what my position would be if we split that David first saw that I really was serious. Then he started blaming me and saying things like 'When will you make up your mind whether you're leaving or not?' or 'You know it's crazy the idea of you going off to be on your own.' I felt awful in the position of being the one to make the decision about our joint problems.

Another common situation is when a partner has serious doubts about the marriage and can talk about them with their partner, but still remains torn about whether the relationship can really be improved, whatever they try together. One feels there is more hope, is more against separating, is less sure than the other. One has been thinking about the issues as they see them and trying to make decisions about the future, doing a sort of inner psychological preparation for changing things. The other finds the problems a threat, and the restitution of the relationship with all its problems the only right answer. Frequently the one who doesn't want the end entreats their partner to stay by promising to change in whatever way is required, which as we've said doesn't usually work in the long term. It doesn't usually inspire the leaving partner's confidence either, because they have some sort of awareness that this isn't the answer. They have no faith in their partner's ability to make real changes, or they have no real complaints because they feel they have no right to have any—they've realised this person just no longer feels right for them, perhaps because they've found someone else. These feelings mean they can't make a real commitment to making things work, though they may try to in an effort to satisfy their partner's need to work on the problems.

These are some of the reasons why facing up to having problems and possibly separating takes most couples a long time. You can see that though it's not surprising it takes so long, it works against your chances of realising you must do something active and positive for your relationship in time for this to work.

Bearing the responsibility

Many couples get stuck because neither wants to make a commitment to work on the issues with the necessary effort or be the one who 'carries the can' about the decision to separate. At the same time, the emotions of the relationship prevent them realising what's going on so they can move towards acknowledging that the problems are their joint responsibility. This is why so many separating couples take flight from the issues and end up apart without ever having tackled the issues together. This cuts off their chances of finding ways to improve their relationship and also of resolving their separation more cooperatively. It's understandable, because lasting improvements *are* hard to achieve, though immensely rewarding if successful. Often people feel unable to make the effort, in case after all that time and trouble they do separate. Most of us aren't sure which way we want to go anyway, and it's hard to take initiative and be responsible amidst considerable inner confusion. Knowing as we do in our heads, if not in our hearts or actions, that relationship problems are joint ones, we don't want to be the one who gets labelled as the one who left the marriage and has to carry the responsibility of being the agent of everyone's hurt. The characteristic 'beating about the bush' over who's really committed to saving the marriage, who most wants the separation, whether to try one more time, often means that real attempts to solve the problems get started too late, or that self-help or counselling programs never get off the ground, or fail.

> We'd had a huge and very traumatic blow-up about finances which shocked us both a lot. When we'd calmed down a bit and realised

> how much damage we'd done to each other we decided to have counselling. We both said we sincerely wanted to get things working well again. After a few meetings though, we discovered we weren't behaving sincerely at all. He was keeping detailed diaries and accounts as if in preparation for the worst—a stormy break up—and I was preventing him doing this properly by taking off for the weekend by myself and looking up old flames. I couldn't acknowledge at the time that I too was sabotaging our attempts at working on the issues. Things just went from bad to worse with us getting more and more angry and suspicious of each other's motives, and yet right to the end we both kept saying we wanted to make it work. Much later I realised that in a way we were both wanting to avoid being the one who took responsibility for being committed to really trying, or being the one who decided to separate.

Having another try

What all these characteristic ways of reacting to doubts about relationships mean is that people generally get around to doing things about the problems too late or in the wrong way. By the time we do, one or other of us is often close to deciding to move out of the relationship. This often means that attempts to solve the problems can't work. They can only work if you are both committed to really trying, and you both put aside threats to separate if it doesn't work and relinquish actively engaging in other relationships.

People give all sorts of reasons for why their marriages failed. They range from very general kinds of things like an inability to communicate, incompatibility, 'we fell out of love' or 'it doesn't feel right', to more specific reasons like 'she had an affair', 'he wouldn't change', 'he walked out on me' and 'constant nagging'. All these are really symptoms, varying in seriousness as far as their emotional impact on the relationship is concerned, of underlying issues, which if addressed properly need not necessarily cost the relationship. We discussed in Chapter 6 how the symptom of an affair needs to be approached if a marriage is to survive it and improve. We recommended in Chapter 4 that if you haven't made a sincere attempt to work on your marriage, you should. If you can't make a real commitment to doing this, then going through the motions will prolong the process of deciding about the relationship even further.

Many relationships of course can, do and often should end, *but the only really sensible reason to part should be that you both made a thorough attempt at understanding why your symptoms developed, and then tried to do things to usefully put this understanding into practice together, and this failed.* However much you want to do this, if your partner doesn't and persists in declining to join with you in making the necessary effort, there isn't much you can do about it. At least you will be able to feel you tried to make a responsible effort yourself.

Accepting your partner's decision

Your separation will be less difficult and painful if, despite your different feelings about the relationship's potential, you manage to acknowledge your differences and work towards separating together, sharing your sadness and mixed feelings.

Unfortunately a common pattern is, as we saw above, for one partner to have more or less decided it's no good, knowing that their partner doesn't want the end. Coping with this is hard, not only for the person who wants to keep the marriage, but also for the one who has to live with the impact of their decision on their partner. The partner who's less able to accept the prospect of the end feels desperate, rejected and convinced that the relationship can work. As events progress, they blame their partner for the change of heart, and seek out every possible way to engage their partner in another try. This position is terribly hard to bear and may last for some time. It makes you go over the past repeatedly looking for things you could have done differently, ways in which you could have changed to satisfy your partner better. You may find yourself believing if only they'd sort themselves out, they'd realise what a lot you had going together, that they're just going through a personal crisis which they'll get over and then change their mind. You may convince yourself that any kind of relationship with your departing partner is better than the loss of it altogether.

The harsh reality is of course that if one person wants out, then however much the other believes in the marriage, they are in fact living with the fantasy of a relationship. A working marriage only exists because two people want to be in it. Sooner, in preference to later, this partner must negotiate for themselves the painful process of coming to terms with this fact and coping with the impending loss of their happiness, definition and well-being which they invested in a relationship that wasn't working. They must deal with their anger at their partner's refusal to reconsider the relationship, and with the true meaning of their dependency on it as distinct from their real love for their partner. If you are in this position it will be very hard for you to accept the fact that partnerships take two. There is little to be gained by entreating your partner to reconsider their decision, but you should restate your feelings to your partner about what you think is possible, and what you'd like to do about the relationship. Do this in as measured a way as you can, regardless of the fact that they disagree with your view, or find your feelings in conflict with theirs.

You will have to face the consequences of your partner's decision and you will survive them. Whilst you may feel that the end of your marriage was decided by your partner, and it wasn't what you wanted, it caused enormous hurt and pain, your adjustment to its loss will in time bring about some useful changes in yourself. Many people end up glad they separated because they've moved on to bigger and better things, even though they were desperately unhappy about the end at the time. *It can take a real challenge like a crisis in a key relationship to motivate some people to look for the first time at the facts of their relationship, and at themselves and their contribution to their circumstances.* Sadly this often means it's too late to apply new awareness thus acquired to the very relationship that prompted this worthwhile goal.

> I was desperately depressed and frightened when Bill finally told me he thought I should leave. He wouldn't say why and even said he still loved me. There were things wrong with the relationship I knew, but I thought I loved him and wanted to have the relationship more than anything else. He wouldn't talk about his reasons and I didn't know how to break the stalemate. He gave me no idea of what I could do to change. I started making all the necessary arrangements to move while he was still giving me confused messages about leaving. Much later I found out some things about the financial side of our nine-year relationship that he'd misled me about which made me angry. They indicated he'd been much less committed

about us than I'd thought. They helped me realise how much I'd been hanging onto the relationship and blinding myself to how bad it really was because of my fears of being rejected and having to face a lonely future. I had accepted a lot of things about him that weren't good enough and I was really amazed later at how frail a person I must be to have accepted and believed in a relationship like this.

Thinking about your options

Your options will of course be determined by what's happened in your own life so far. Here's a range of choices along with some recommendations about them.

- To do nothing and hope for the best. This is obviously a passive stance, which works for some people, but it's unlikely to help you achieve your hopes for the best. If you're sufficiently motivated to be reading this book, this option probably won't be good enough for you. It may give you time to get to the point where your partner wants to do something with you about the relationship, if they don't now. Meanwhile you should be doing something more towards the relationship than just waiting.
- To put up with things as they are. This is similarly passive and it may be what you think you should do if you've made some attempt to address the problems and haven't got anywhere. *It makes no sense to prolong an unsatisfactory relationship indefinitely if it can't work, just to avoid a sense of failure, or for the sake of the children.* So ask yourself whether being a martyr to the cause of sustaining a marriage is really good for you or anyone else in the long-run.
- To work on the relationship actively together. Start with reconsidering Chapter 4 together, and make a plan. As we said earlier this is the only option that will tell you whether you can improve things or not. When you know that despite a genuine effort you can't, then this is a sensible and mutual basis on which to make a separation decision.
- To work on the issues, but your partner won't do this with you. Continue to talk to your partner at frequent intervals about

your concerns. Don't be put off trying to get talking by their non-response. Read and think on your own, and go on trying to do things yourself for the relationship in positive ways. Later on, but not too much later, reconsider your other options.

- To compromise by changing your priorities and your expectations. Only you can decide whether you are willing to accept your relationship as it is. Changing your expectations is a matter of deciding whether what you think you hoped for is realistic, especially when you're contemplating leaving one relationship for another newer one. Before you alter your expectations or your priorities you should ask yourself whether they are achievable, realistic or dispensible, and whether it's you, the relationship or your partner that's responsible for your feeling you aren't getting what you want.
- To work on your own personal issues so you know more about how you function in relationships and how this affects your partner. This is always worthwhile. In a relationship that's working well you do this for each other together. If your partner doesn't want to do this with you, it may well help you to do it on your own by reading, thinking and trying new ways of functioning, perhaps with the help of counselling.
- To take some time out of the relationship to sort your thoughts out in a trial separation. Unless you do something structured and active while you're away on your own, just being apart won't give you the answers. And unless you both discuss and agree to the idea, and understand what a temporary separation is supposed to be achieving, you may do some irretrievable emotional damage to your partner and hence to the relationship. More on trial separations in Chapter 8.
- To separate. Don't do this unless you've tried to work things out together and are reasonably sure you can't. If you haven't done this and still want to leave, make sure you've had a period of time with your partner knowing as much as you can tell them about the reasons for your decision and accepting their reactions to it.
- To separate together. If you've both acknowledged you must separate, keep talking together about your feelings about it (you'll each have some regrets and uncertainties). This will help you disengage from your time together with better understanding and mutual respect, and help you make all the

practical decisions about the future amicably. You could benefit from separation counselling to help this disengaging process.
- To let your partner go. If your partner has decided they are leaving you don't have too many options, however much you may want to persuade them to stay and try again. But you do owe it to yourself and the relationship to make clear your feelings and hopes to your partner.

While you're still together, compromising or embarking on self-help or counselling continues to be an option available to you. Up to a certain point in a deteriorating relationship it is possible to reverse the process and improve things. But there seems to come a point of no return, at the stage when a couple have tried to improve things by bargaining and have repeatedly let each other down so that gradually one or other loses faith in the relationship.

Once you've separated, your relationship will never be the same again, and there's a real risk that feelings of hurt and resentment may be set in train which exclude some other options. Separating is rather final, so think carefully. *The longer you spend together trying to face the reality of your own and/or your partner's doubts, the better you'll both be able to cope with separating if that has to happen.* However much you don't want to part, at least then you've had time to try and get used to the idea of being on your own before the parting. And if you're the 'prime mover' about separating, the surer you'll be likely to feel. While you're together you'll have readier opportunities to try and explain what's happened and understand each other's point of view. More on 'Clean breaks' in Chapter 8.

Knowing when to quit

Because we want to avoid the pain of ending a relationship we allow a lot of unpleasant and even unbearable things to go on, not knowing whether we should be enduring these or whether they are a sign that it should end. You'll remember that one of the main reasons for this book was because so many people get stuck not knowing what to do, whether they really can or really can't make it work. Here's a check list to help you find the answer to this. Go through each item and answer the ones that apply to you as clearly and accurately as you can.

- Are you sure you've really tried to talk together about why the marriage isn't working for you? And listened to your partner's point of view? If you don't get a very helpful response, don't give up trying to get one. Leave the topic for a while, but keep bringing up your need to discuss things. You may think you're getting nowhere but all your efforts will contribute in some way to your partner's acceptance that you're seriously concerned.
- Are you sure it's the marriage that's the trouble? Perhaps you're expecting too much from it—another person can't possibly be the source of all the personal fulfilment you need in order to be a contented and satisfied individual. Are there some changes you could make in your life to help you feel more in charge and freer to generate your own excitement, which would also help you appraise this relationship in a more balanced way? (See Chapter 1.)
- If you badly want the marriage to continue and your partner doesn't, are you mistaking your love for them, your profound and distressing feelings of wanting to preserve the relationship despite their unhappiness, for your own dependency and insecurity about change?
- Have you talked to someone about your situation, such as a trusted friend? Preferably one who gets you thinking about yourself and doesn't just tell you what they think you want to hear.
- Have you talked about the possibility of both meeting together with a counsellor? Expect a little resistance from your partner to this idea if they've showed reluctance to talk with you; try to help your partner understand, from what you've found out, what counselling is and isn't, in case some misconceptions are affecting their willingness to try.
- Have you given your marriage enough time to weather the normal everyday stresses of things like job changes, house moves, new parenthood, financial pressures, accidents etc? Are either of you blaming your dissatisfactions on these events, rather than on your joint ability to share and support each other about them?
- Have you really asked yourself what you might be contributing to the unsatisfactory partnership? What you could do yourself to improve things? In other words, are you taking responsibility yourself for *your* half of the marriage?

- How realistic are you being about the future with your new love? Have you honestly addressed whether it's valid to compare what your relationship feels like after several years with what your new, untested one feels like now?
- Will acknowledging your marital failure and doing something about it—separating—conflict with your spiritual and religious convictions about commitment to marriage and parenthood? How will this really affect you? What will be the effects on both you and your partner's families?
- How realistic are you being about the future on your own? Is separating something that you can really do, when it comes to considering practical things like finances, housing, child-care and other family obligations?

Once you've considered all these, you may be a little surer that there's going to have to be a separation, whether you instigate it or your partner does. Or you may be surer that it's worth staying together longer and making some undertakings or compromises so that the marriage continues while you see if these work.

Deciding which route to take at a major turning point in your relationship is not something you can do overnight. You should expect to experience a fairly lengthy period of indecision punctuated by times of relative certainty, a sense of hopelessness and personal failure, apparent improvements, or just drifting along not feeling too unhappy about things. You won't wake up one morning knowing for certain that you can recapture your former happiness by making some changes, or that you absolutely must split up. Decisions in relationships are hardly ever this clear-cut. And the consequences of your decisions are so far-reaching that it's wise not to make them in a rush.

When you feel reasonably certain that you know which way you want to head—to try and make it work together, to make do, or to separate—you must accept that 'reasonably certain' will probably be the surest you'll get! You'll be ambivalent and anxious about what you've decided to do. This needn't prevent you making the necessary commitment to the course you've decided to take. Whatever steps you've taken to go about things in the best and most informed way, the reality is that relationship decisions are seldom black and white. You'll both have some regrets and uncertainties. You should accept and acknowledge these as to be expected. Even though you may both have acknowledged that you're going to have to part, it's unlikely that you'll both be equally ready for it when the time comes, as we've seen. This will mean your feelings and your partner's will be different when you actually split and you'll both be in for a tricky, sad and frustrating time for at least a few months and probably longer, while you both adjust to the changes.

So facing up to separation is a gradual process which will affect you both in various ways, and they'll seldom coincide. You'll both feel sad, angry, hurtful, loving and frustrated towards each other at different times. As a result, you'll find you drift further and further apart because it's hard to talk. When the time comes for something to be done about the relationship it's become impossible to cooperate about its future. Your partner may have grown remote and moody, spending less time at home and unwilling to discuss things with you; perhaps privately thinking a separation might come; you may be generally dissatisfied but not really questioning the marriage; or perhaps thinking about separation but unable to see it as a real option, for practical reasons as well as emotional ones.

If it's separation that think you face, then your next task is to start considering how to approach it. *You can manage your separation better if you are sensibly prepared.* Once you've arrived at an informed decision about separating, you'll need some help with mastering your separation effectively. Knowing how it's likely to affect everybody (and particularly you) will be a great help. The better prepared and stronger you feel, the better off everyone will be.

8 Facing up to separating

When either of you has decided to separate, and therefore can no longer consider the option of staying together and trying to make changes, the next phase of your relationship begins. The decision is made, and it's out in the open between you. In some ways the hardest part is over. The cards are on the table and you have a decision, whether you like it or not. Neither of you *will* wholeheartedly like it, but you've got through some of the uncertainty, the doubts, the discomfort of decision-making and the painful discussions. The process of disengaging from your life together is under way and you're a step nearer to a more resolved and positive future.

You don't just end a relationship when you change addresses. Even when you don't have children, you continue having a relationship of sorts with your partner for a time, which may involve getting back together perhaps more than once, before it all seems really final. When there are children, then of course you are bound to continue a relationship with each other, one that has to change, as we saw in Chapter 5, from being disenchanted partners into becoming communicating co-parents so that your children can adjust to you being separated and later having new partners.

Steering through the period between deciding and parting

There are some advantages to having a period together once the decision to separate has been made and communicated about. Couples often do this anyway in an attempt to iron out further any possible doubts, and for practical reasons such as needing to organise alternative accommodation for one or both partners. It's a difficult time, and in one sense there's a feeling (at least for one person) that having made the decision it's best to make a quick and clean break and get on with a new life. But staying together for a while after the decision, however uncomfortable it may feel, does give time for useful (if painful) exchanges about the reasons and the feelings you're each having. This allows the process of disengaging from your life together to begin, which is an important first step to adjusting to it all. It makes for a more shared feeling about the responsibility for what's happening than if you part immediately the decision is in the open. It also minimises the tendency to blame and point-score. It will help you with all the decision-making you now face about joint responsibilities of children, assets and belongings. It enables you to more jointly prepare the children for what's about to happen.

However much you may feel a clean and swift break will be best in the long-term, be sure to consider whether you think this is because it's going to be easier for you, if you're the one who's wanting to separate most. *You have a responsibility to do whatever will make your decision more bearable to your family; an obligation to give your partner the opportunity to express their feelings about your decision to you, giving them the chance to understand better why you made it.* Many partners are left after a split up preoccupied to an unhelpful extent with not knowing what went wrong, and under great pressure to go over events to try and find answers. They may feel driven to find the answers from family and friends (who don't really know what went on in the relationship). *Painful and difficult though it is, and however much you'd prefer to avoid doing it, you can help your partner and yourself to separate and adjust sooner with better acceptance if you do this rather than withdraw.* Depending on your position about separating, you will want to make protests, denials, entreaties and promises, or you will have to respond to these somehow without being too destructive. You'll find yourself going over aspects of the past, often more than once, and asking many questions of each other. Try to see all this as a necessary part of the process of mourning the end of the relationship.

You may be feeling guilty, uncertain of the future and angry at how difficult it's all been. Perhaps you're worried that your uncertainties might be interpreted by your partner as a sign of hope, which is another common reason for people wanting to cut themselves off completely. Your partner may be feeling abandoned, unsupported, insecure, hurt and angry. Expect these feelings as a normal reaction to a major life event that has an uncertain future. Very few separations are emotionally tranquil, because, even when the need to separate is more or less mutual, there are always mixed feelings.

The loss of a relationship is a kind of bereavement and we pass through a series of emotional stages, which are characteristic of grief reactions, as we adjust to the loss. First we experience feelings of shock and denial. We say 'It can't be true that I'm not going to be a married person any more, that I'm going to be on my own', or 'This can't be happening to me!' Paradoxically, you might think, feelings of denial are also experienced by the partner who is the 'prime mover' over the decision to split.

> We had a difficult time once the fact of having to separate was out in the open. I suppose everybody does. I wanted to leave more than Ian did, and we'd managed to work out a timetable and told the children quite successfully together. But I still found myself doing things like thinking about redecorating the living room in the near future even though I was leaving! I guess I was denying the full reality of what I'd decided to do, and didn't want to look at the full implications of my decision. Looking back on this time now, I can see it wouldn't have helped Ian because it would have made him think I was going to change my mind and stay. He was trying to pretend it wasn't going to happen as it was, talking about future plans for our next holiday together, and behaving in most ways as if nothing had changed.

The next stage in adjusting to the loss of the relationship is the period of angry protest, where the 'How could you do this to me after all I've done for the marriage all these years?' and 'How could you so disappoint me that I'm forced to leave you and break up the family?' These kinds of questions come up, often punctuated by angry fault-finding. However civilised and patient you're trying to be, you'll both probably feel angry and annoyed at times. Don't fight these feelings, they're normal, so acknowledge them and work at handling them the best way.

Try to communicate your angry feelings to each other, seeing it as a necessary part of disengaging from your life together. The way to do this usefully without being destructive is to omit language that is accusing and apportions blame. Remember, in a responsible relationship *you* are the one who creates and owns their feelings, including your angry and accusing ones which are sure to surface as you try to justify the decision you've had to make. When you're discussing the relationship and the impending separation and things look like getting out of hand, this is the kind of talk you should be aiming for to help achieve better understanding between you:

> When you do this (for example, don't seem to be able to show you understand my position) in this situation (when we're trying to discuss how much time I spend at work), I tend to react in this kind of way (I feel misunderstood, undermined and unsupported). My frustration is my problem, for responding to you this way, not yours. I've tried for a long time to deal with my reactions to you and this issue more effectively, and I find unfortunately that try as I might, I can't. I can't find a way to give to our relationship what is necessary to solve this problem and others, so I've failed, and the only solution I'm able to find for us both is for me to go. Try not to see it as my finding fault with you, you are you, and I can't ask you to stop being what you are just because I can't find my own solution to this joint issue between us, etc.

Notice that this is honest, authentic talk which accepts responsibility for aspects of the relationship, rather than pinpointing behaviour faults on the part of one partner only. You may remember it as 'levelling' from Chapter 4. Try to keep to this kind of way of presenting the issues if you possibly can. Don't expect your partner to immediately respond to your efforts in an accepting way. *You're aiming to give them the best opportunity to do this, but remember that even though you're trying to be honest and responsible about what's happening, your partner is still bound to react emotionally to your communications.* They haven't been doing as much preparing for separating as you have and so they'll feel threatened and anxious. They are bound to feel that they themselves and the relationship you had together are being rejected. Your position is that you're having to leave the relationship because you've found some aspects of it unworkable despite the good things. This isn't the same as you committing a single-minded deliberate act of rejection. It may be hard for your partner to see it this way.

> We had a fairly torrid time preparing for separating. Whenever we tried to discuss things she would end up crying, and I'd get furious with her and want to walk out and slam the door. I couldn't count the number of times we'd tried to talk about how we can't have a relationship without two of us. If I wanted out that was it, why couldn't she see this? I would get really stirred up when she disintegrated, thinking she was deliberately trying to make it all even more difficult for me.
>
> Then I decided to try a different approach because I really didn't want to turn into a door-slamming type, and I wanted to try and show her that I sympathised, but I was also angry. I read something about fight control and tried it. I made a time with her to talk some more and started off by asking her to really listen till I'd finished. I told her how I was feeling about everything from a list I'd prepared. It included things like the fact that when she cried I got angry and my feeling angry made me unable to appear as if I was taking any notice of her position, which I imagined made me seem harsh and uncaring. Then I said that I also found it hard to tell her how guilty and confused I felt because I was afraid that it would appear to her as if, having decided to leave her, I also wanted her sympathy about my decision. This is a pretty crazy thing to ask from someone whose only response could be: if you're confused and you can't handle the guilt then don't leave! But not telling her why I was acting the way I was wasn't helping either. After this session I think we were more understanding of each other's point of view and didn't seem to need to talk so much. It was as if some of our talking had been serving the purpose of allowing us to have another little go at being angry at each other.
>
> Looking back on this time, I'm glad I 'hung in there' and tried to keep talking with her rather than just walking out, although that would have been much easier for me.

Then, characteristically comes the bargaining stage which serves to sustain the relationship with offers like 'can you come over and fix the car, I'll cook you a meal, I don't expect you're eating properly'. If you get stuck at the bargaining stage you may find yourself doing potentially damaging things later on like obstructing the children's contact with your partner until money is forthcoming from them, or until they cooperate with you in some other way. In a sense it's a way of sustaining a hope that the relationship isn't really dead for a bit longer. A conflict-ridden relationship seems better than none at all. Sometimes this stage degenerates into provocative and recriminative behaviour, a need to punish for past omissions, for deserting, for causing current suffering. The leaving partner responds by insistently demanding a rationality and detachment on the part of their partner that emotionally they are quite unable to give, because of their anger, hurt and their need to blame. *Understanding that this may be what's going on may help you to avoid doing things that sustain this conflict or whip it up further.*

Finally, the reality of the separation and its permanence really sinks in at last and depression often sets in. You finally have had to face the facts. For example, that your dream of being separated did not prepare you for the reality of life on your own, the loss of the bits of the relationship you valued more than you realised, a sense of isolation and uncertainty. The reality of having failed and the resulting damaged sense of worth will come home to you as you struggle to adjust to your separation and to the fact that there's nothing you can do to change it. These feelings may continue and fluctuate for quite a time after you separate, before you can accept it all and get on with adjusting to life apart.

What to do as a couple while you separate emotionally

- Never abandon your attempts at continued authentic communication about your position, needs and feelings with your partner. Not communicating is a stalemate. Remember that however frustrating it is, talking always provides the chance of getting somewhere useful or at least somewhere different.
- Don't give up on your attempts to talk about the decisions you must make for the future, even if you have to give up on talking about the relationship.
- Acknowledge to each other (yes, again!) that it's hard, and that you each have feelings and reactions that make you say hurtful or misleading things at times.

- If your discussions become really wound up and unproductive, suggest you conclude the discussion for the moment and resume it when you've each had a chance to come to grips with what the problem is that's firing up your talks. Try not to leave attempts at problem-solving without some kind of closure, by acknowledging for example that it's unhelpful to continue for the moment and saying what issues need addressing further, for example.
- When you reconvene, you should say to your partner exactly how you feel in response to things they do or say, or positions they adopt on issues. Like the example above, this is 'levelling' talk as we described in Chapter 4.
- If your talks increasingly tend to degenerate into destructive arguments, acknowledge this and agree to find a person who could mediate for you.
- Consider the possible benefits of some separation counselling together, if either of you are stuck and unable to accept the situation. Even if you think there's no hope of reaching acceptance of your separation together, a trained person may be able to help you do this. Nothing is worse for a person distraught at the ending of a relationship than to feel they didn't get the opportunity to try and understand.

What to do for yourself

- Accept that your feelings will chop and change a bit. Accept your bad and mixed feelings about yourself, your partner, and your separation.
- Limit how much time you spend going over the past, because you can't undo it, and it often makes you feel more sorry for yourself than is helpful.
- Don't allow yourself to overindulge in blaming your partner. It never gets you anywhere useful. Remember that blaming is something we do to avoid being responsible for our circumstances and taking action, to justify our decisions, and to give vent to our anger.
- Accept that what you're facing is difficult, but at the same time don't allow yourself to believe the world really has fallen in, or that you'll never be able to cope. You will. But be realistic

—separating won't be easy, however thoroughly and skillfully you're trying to manage it.

- Try to remind yourself that a partnership can't exist just because you want it to, or you think it will be able to once your partner realises what's best for them, or gets themselves 'sorted out'. Repeat to them how you feel about the future and ask for explanations. The more information you can get about how love has changed for your partner, the sooner you'll adjust to it all. Allow yourself to be angry and depressed. Talk to someone about it at length, because you could probably do with some extra support.
- Marriage is of course as legal as any other kind of partnership, so find out some sound facts about the legal consequences of separating from a self-help product or from a specialist divorce lawyer.
- If you are beset by feelings of guilt about your decision and about how your partner is going to cope, remind yourself that if you're at least trying to mastermind your separation as sensibly and sympathetically as you can, you'll be taking useful action to relieve your guilt.
- Don't be too hard on yourself. You are responsible for your decisions, actions and feelings, but only to a certain extent for their consequences. *You can only take a certain amount of responsibility on your shoulders for another's reactions and adjustments*. These belong to them and your responsibility for them can only go so far.

Trial separations

Some people deal with uncertainty about their decision by trying out a separation. They go 'out there' to see what it feels like, as if something will tell them it's the right or the wrong move. You can only do a certain amount of productive thinking about the relationship out there on your own. You may find out how awful or okay living on your own feels in the short term. This may tell you that there's no need to stay in the relationship just because it's too scary out there. You might discover that it's easier than you thought to find a flat and be on your own etc. *This discovery isn't the same as finding out whether your relationship could be made to work*. You may feel relief through having taken some action, but don't mistake this for a sign that you're necessarily better off apart. Trying out living out of your relationship won't tell you whether you can live in it.

Others say they're leaving for a while to sort things out, get some breathing space, have a break from the relationship. They mean this in a sense, but are often disguising their real intention to part permanently so as to soften the blow. It's an expression of their own ambivalence at the time, and it can be very misleading for their partner. Most couples who separate stay separated. This is because for some, separating is the right decision. But for others it is because once apart, adjustments begin. The reasonable comfort of new living circumstances along with the relief and novelty of feeling more in charge of their lives is taken as meaning it was right to separate, and they may as well continue with it. Adjustments also begin for their partner, so they may be less willing to have you back than you assumed they'd be. You may therefore find you've closed some doors when you embark on a trial separation, unless you've discussed and agreed to the purposes and time span of the proposed separation and what contact you'll have for what purpose during it.

After about a year of trying to discuss our relationship productively, I couldn't really say we'd solved anything, just tied ourselves in ever more complicated knots. We had to have periods where talking about 'us' was disallowed, to ease the enormous pressure of our preoccupation with ourselves. After a few false starts, Alan eventually moved out, though I never thought he'd ever have the courage to. He insisted it was for a trial period to think things over. He came round every day, took me to work, had meals with us. It was a most frustrating time for us. I felt I'd learnt a lot about my needs and behaviour, and changed from originally wanting to separate to wanting to stay together and work things out. So I kept wanting to ask Alan whether he'd made up his mind, how much longer he wanted, and all he would say was that he couldn't answer that. We were just as stuck as we were before we'd separated! Only now my dilemma was how long to let this go on for. If I try to get on with my separate life, must I stop seeing him so much? Will this push him further away? I spent enormous amounts of time going over things he'd said and done, trying to look for indications which would help me know what to do. But I never seemed to get anywhere with him when I tried to get him to clarify things he'd said. After a while I came to realise that he wasn't going to give me any answers or come back no matter what I did, and that he'd just used the trial separation thing to make the transition easier for himself, whether he realised this or not.

Getting back together

A temporary separation can make things seem clearer for some people, but be prepared to jointly make some firm commitments about what you're going to do for the future of your partnership when you reunite. Otherwise you may find that your relationship resumes where it left off rather quickly. *Getting back together and finding it works is at least as hard as deciding to separate and finding that works.* Of course you can have another go if your partner agrees, but you can be sure that none of the problems that caused you to part in the first place will necessarily have changed, although the relief and comfort of being back together and a 'fresh start' will give you a nice positive glow for a while. Before you parted you probably had a rosy picture of the relief and freedom that having decided and done it would give you. The reality out there on your own is about taking on the huge adjustments of loneliness, guilt, sadness, boredom etc. You may find you want to go back because it's lonely, rather than because you really want to make the relationship work. Or you've discovered how much of the relationship you've been taking for granted. So don't reconcile expecting it all to just happen. *You must make some sincere undertakings together about what you're both going to do to ensure you don't slide back towards where you were before.* It's a good idea to discuss reconciling a few times before you actually do. Work out an agenda together, exchange what you think you've each learnt from being apart.

Decisions about children and finances

The big decision to separate is of course just the beginning of a series of further decisions with their own far-reaching consequences, some of which you'll probably already have been thinking about.

The first one is usually who's going to live where. Most often this is a decision about which of you leaves the established home, and of course the presence of children tends to have a bearing on the foreseeable options. We began considering the practical aspects of living arrangements in Chapter 5, and we'll take this further here.

Sometimes the partner who's the keenest on separating feels they must be the one who leaves. When it's the partner who currently has the major caretaking role with young children, then it may make more practical sense for the reluctant partner to leave. This is hard to arrange sensitively, and certainly preparing for it is going to take time. If you believe your marriage can work and you love your partner, it's tough to leave your home, children and emotional security as well as your partner.

In many, if not most, families the children, especially if they're young, stay with their mother. This isn't because mothers necessarily have any biological superiority in parenting, but because often she has been doing most of the caretaking at least in the early years, because she started off doing it during pregnancy, birth and baby's early infancy. It's for you to decide what's best for your children in your particular circumstances. More and more fathers are participating in parenting nowadays than ever before, but many couples still want Mum to be Mum at least for the first years, and because Mum has often interrupted her career with pregnancy anyway. So she gets good at it, and not only does it therefore make sense for her to continue having a major role with the children, but often her greater day-to-day involvement with them means their attachment to her is strong, particularly in the early years of their lives. And it's still the case that for many couples Mum can't earn as much as Dad so with increasing financial commitments it merely makes sense.

There are two principles which should govern how the question of the children should be decided. There are several reasons which parents may mistakenly rely on which shouldn't. We'll discuss these in turn.

You two are the children's parents, so the starting point for decisions that affect their wellbeing is that *you are the best people to decide what's right for them.* Talk about this together, in as balanced a way as you can given that your emotions about separating will affect what you personally might prefer for them. You're aiming to work out cooperatively what arrangements are going to best meet their needs, not yours. This is the second principle, that their emotional wellbeing should come first, and not yours.

The children's continuing contact with both of you after you've separated is important to their adjustment as we saw in Chapter 5. Try and make a plan for how and when they're going to see both of you. Knowing how important this is going to be for them will help you decide on the arrangements.

Now for the reasons that shouldn't override your decision-making. In your efforts to work out new living arrangements that will best serve the children's needs, *don't rely on them to tell you how their needs are best met.* This is what parents should be deciding for their children, based on their knowledge of their children's individual temperaments, stage of development and what is feasible from a practical point of view. Once children know there is to be a separation they should be encouraged to express themselves about it and the arrangements if they appear to want to. You should field their comments and apparent wishes in a supportive way (so they feel involved and noticed), but not in such a way that they feel *they* are making such major decisions as a choice between one parent at the expense of the other. It's too much of a burden for a young mind to have to grapple with decisions and choices about the two people they're totally dependent upon. Tell them you're listening, but that you parents are going to decide what's best for everyone, or that you're going together to talk to someone about it. Older children can be involved more actively in the discussions. But remember, children can't foresee what you two living apart is going to feel like *and must be protected from being involved, even unwittingly on your part, in anything that might feel like making choices or taking sides.*

Many parents feel there is an established right and wrong thing to do about the children, which child welfare experts or lawyers should advise them about, or which they are obliged to abide by. Informing yourself about the facts from the experts is fine and is often helpful and reassuring, but you'll most likely not find a clear answer. Everybody's circumstances are so unique that a right answer cannot readily be given from outside the family. In any event, there are no authorities 'out there' requiring you to do things a certain way just because you're separating. They only exist to make decisions for you when you can't make your own and *have* to use them, because your discussions continually fail to result in satisfactory agreements.

So the overriding principle is that *what you can decide yourselves is going to be what works, because it sustains joint parental responsibility and continued contribution from both of you to their lives*. That's what they want and need most. The importance of decisions and parenting plans that promote continued joint involvement in family responsibilities, despite separations, is a principle that is reflected throughout welfare agencies. The importance of children's continued contact with both their parents goes hand in hand with this.

When thinking about who lives where, some people get stuck fearing that they my lose a share in the eventual settlement of the family property by moving out. This can be a real stumbling-block. You should try to discuss what makes sense for the family and make some undertakings about how jointly acquired assets are most fairly apportioned, ready for when the time comes to do this. You could make your undertakings more formal if you think you need this security.

In the emotional turmoil of preparing to separate you may find you get caught up with rights, fairness and entitlements. For example, you may find you're feeling so hurt and damaged, and threatened by the prospects of singleness that you want to punish your partner by hanging on to as many assets or demanding as much for child maintenance as you can, or by obstructing a financial agreement for as long as possible. You may be feeling so guilty that you'd rather surrender your claim to a fair share as a way of making up for your part in what's happened. This may mean you agree to things that make your future harder for you or that you regret later. *Think about what seems fair and considerate, and weigh this up against what your respective immediate needs and earning prospects are*. Also consider what your own values and inclinations to be generous or self-protective are—what you think you can live with. Make a provisional plan, discuss it, think about it over a period of time and then meet again.

If you still can't agree, then see a divorce lawyer. They can advise you what your rights and entitlements are likely to be in the eyes of the law, based on similar known circumstances and how the principles of justice are applied in courts. (They cannot advise you as to how any one of a range of settlements might rest with you emotionally. This is for you to decide and then, if necessary, instruct them to act accordingly on your behalf to achieve what you want.) If your partner seems to want to persist in being unreasonable, you must then decide if it's worth your while in the long and the short term to stick to what you believe and have been advised is fair, and take your case to court. Beware of 'going for broke' just for the sake of retaliating because you're angry at their refusal to cooperate. But consider also the effects of 'selling yourself short', although you may decide it's worth it.

Responsible planning

Here's a list containing some reminders and further recommendations, which you can approach as an 'action plan for a responsible separation'.

- Do whatever is humanly possible to keep amicable communication going between you and your partner, even if you have to tone down your feelings and compromise frequently. This mightn't seem fair, and you'll probably find it hard to control the urge to point-score or rake up past disappointments. Doing this won't help your discussions.
- Try to take responsibility *yourselves* for your changing family circumstances. Relatives, friends and new partners can offer you useful support and guidance, but your separation arrangements are for you to decide about, just as arranging to get married was your responsibility.
- Make a list of all the practical things that have to be decided, like who is going to do what with the children, who's going to pay for what and how this is going to happen; how are you going to divide up your belongings including your credit cards and sentimental items. This is a time for thinking and planning comprehensively so as to prepare yourself in advance for all the decisions you may face, not just the ones with the most immediate priority.
- Before a meeting with your partner, write a list of what you want to say, to help keep yourself logical and not too emotional. Be prepared for sadness, guilt and anger to often interfere with your best intentions.
- Be prepared to face considerable adjustments to your finances and standards of living, however unfair this might seem.

Obviously being apart is going to cost more, and may force you to consider new income sources. If you don't want to be separated, it may be difficult for you to offer material and financial support to your partner for their future apart from you.

- Don't involve the children in your adult differences. They'll most likely have sensed something isn't quite right. When you have a reasonably firm plan, try to present it to them jointly, before you separate. We discussed how to do this in Chapter 5.
- Explain the future day-to-day arrangements (not the finances) to the children in a way that shows that you both cooperated with the plan. Don't give them too much choice about visiting arrangements, certainly to begin with and especially if they're fairly young.
- Don't be in a rush to introduce new partners to the children. They'll need *you* right now and will be confused, angry and resentful about new partners to begin with, and may blame the parent who has a new person in their life for being the destroyer of the family. Consider the advantages to them of leaving new partners' direct involvement till later when things have settled down a bit. More on new families in Chapter 9.
- Have as many discussions over and over again as you can, because later on you need to feel you've tried absolutely everything to help it all go as smoothly as possible, leaving you both with some understanding about it all. Remember, talking together can lead somewhere useful, even if it hasn't so far.
- Stop and think from time to time whether you're doing all that's reasonably possible to look after the interests of your partner and the children.

Seeking legal help

It's surprising how many people haven't ever thought much about what our legal system is for when it comes to marriage, or about the principles by which it operates and their effects. When a person seeks the advice of a lawyer they first of all want information about their position in the eyes of the law. Asking someone else for advice about your family is fine, but don't leave behind your own good sense, system of values and sense of responsibility about working this out for yourself. You may have to be guided and seek representation, especially if you're stuck, unable to agree on anything, or feel you must defend your partner's claim, but know that this is what you're doing and ask as many questions about the system and its workings as you can. A lawyer's job is to tell you the facts such as what you have to do to get divorced, whether moving out of the family home could prejudice your claim to your rightful share in its value, what is a reasonable maintenance figure etc. Don't lose sight of the fact that a lawyer's advice will be governed by precedents set in legal cases which by definition are extremely contentious cases to have required formal judgement. Their proper professional duty is to offer you protection from the worst possible kind of tactics your partner might resort to, and to engage on your behalf in a strategy aimed at you getting the most out of each other, if this is what you want to do.

Quite obviously this is hardly conducive to cooperative relations within a family, especially a troubled one. As we suggested earlier, it's a good idea to find out, either from an approved information package or an accredited specialist in family law, some basic information about the legal side of separating from the procedural point of view. But beware of relinquishing your independence and autonomy about decision-making over children and property (unless there are extremes of conflict between you, or your partner has initiated proceedings and you feel this obliges you to hire a lawyer yourself). You may not be in a very good position to give sensible instructions because, for example, your emotions are interfering with your ability to determine your children's real needs, or your feelings may be clouding your vision about what may be workable in the long-term because you're wanting fairness at all costs now. You may find that instructing a lawyer to protect your rights and interests sets you off on a course of action which has a polarising effect between you and your partner, making things antagonistic and confrontational, not to mention costly. Because you hire a lawyer to represent you and you only, you may be advised not to even speak to your partner about the joint responsibilities you have to deal with, while they are engaged in negotiating them for you on your behalf.

It has long been considered customary to appoint a lawyer when marriages break up. Yes, we do sometimes feel our position as a partner and parent has been violated and that we might be exposed or exploited, and we feel insecure and uncertain about the future etc. We may feel we want protection. The legal system may be able to help you, but think about whether you are making an informed and sensible decision about using it, aware of its methods and their likely consequences.

There are clear signs that the inadvisability of embarking on legal methods for solving divorce and separation problems is being really recognised in social welfare law and policy. This is because the welfare of children is best served by encouraging cooperative responsibility in parents, and this tends to be undermined or is usurped by legal intervention. There is a new emphasis in most English-speaking cultures on self-responsibility about family break up. There are more opportunities for conciliatory methods of problem-solving, disincentives to litigation, expansion of non-adversarial alternatives like counselling and mediation services. They are designed to encourage the use of alternatives to the legal system for solving family disagreements.

All this is not to say that the law has no proper role to play in family dispute resolution, but rather that in its traditional adversarial form, it should be reserved for use with the most contentious problems after all other less adversarial methods have persistently failed. You should inform yourself as fully as possible before you embark on giving instructions or following advice. This is a sound principle that applies whenever you seek the assistance of an expert of any kind.

Coping with the emotions of separating

The reasons why you couldn't make it work, as well as the sadness of it all, will make it hard to do the necessary talking to reorganise your life as 'separates' and perhaps as parents too. Many ongoing questions will continue to preoccupy you even though you think you're sure. You'll want to understand more clearly what went wrong (especially if you feel hurt and abandoned because you were 'left'), how you've changed since the beginning of the relationship, how you can effectively get on with being single, how you can approach your next relationship differently, why you feel disenchanted with the very idea of close relationships. Most importantly you'll want to know, whichever of you it was who made the final decision to part, how to manage the complicated business of making it all go as smoothly as possible for you both, and particularly for the children.

What you go through emotionally will be affected by your own unique circumstances, and how much you could talk about it together. If you were the keenest to separate, you're probably better prepared emotionally, because you've been planning it. Nevertheless, expect to feel disappointed, lonely, guilty, depressed and inadequate, as well as relieved and pleased to have had the strength to take charge of your life. If your partner left you, expect to be 'in shock' even if you knew it had to come. You'll feel disbelief, rage, despair, loneliness and self-pity. You may badly want your partner back, warts and all, for a long time to come.

Try not to involve the children too much in your sadness. They'll need to see you as strong and consistent, not frail and disorganised. It will get better. Try not to assume your partner is having an easy time of it. They'll be going through a range of difficult transitions however sure they were they wanted the separation. If the children are staying mainly with you, your partner is bound to be feeling sad about losing contact with them. Expect to find yourself going over the past a lot. This is because you'll be preoccupied with why it all went wrong, why it hurts so much, what you could have done to prevent it, or could still do to make amends and try again. You've been rejected so you're bound to feel inadequate and depressed. At other times you'll be angry and find yourself blaming your partner for everything.

You should expect to feel angry. *A necessary part of recovering from a personal failure is convincing yourself that it wasn't all your fault. But attributing blame doesn't get you very far. Being bathed in self-criticism isn't useful either, but expect both these feelings to affect you over the coming months*. Blaming yourself and your partner more or less at different times will affect you both as you try to adjust to it all. As we shall see in Chapter 9, experiencing these emotions is a necessary part of adjusting to and recovering from major changes.

If all these warnings about difficult emotions and challenging adjustments seem daunting and negative, take heart! Anticipating the hurdles you're likely to face equips you better to cope with them when they confront you, because you're more understanding and prepared. And if you've thought about most of the points that have been made and tried to put them into practice, you'll be readier to take on the emotional adjustments of having had to separate, and be more contented with your decision.

9 New directions

By now you may be closer to a decision. Perhaps you've made one, communicated it to your partner and tried to talk it through together despite the bad and sad feelings. Or maybe you've had a period when you both acknowledged the difficulties and tried to solve them perhaps with outside help, and have had to conclude your relationship can't be made to work. Or it's been decided for you by your partner, and you've tried to discuss ways to improve things to no avail, so you've somehow managed to face it and get on with separating. Or perhaps you're still thinking about which route to take forward in the relationship.

Wherever you've got to, you'll need to anticipate what comes after separating. The next set of hurdles will involve some of these challenges: dealing with your feelings which will chop and change over the next months and years, coping with the demands of shared parenting, how to get circulating again, or maybe how to avoid relationships for a while, how to reconstruct a strong sense of self after a big knock, and to manage singleness, new partnerships and new families. The tasks of starting over are beginning.

Good mourning

How we navigate these hurdles will be very much governed by our own attitudes and feelings about life in general and our separation in particular, which we often carry with us for some time, whether we acknowledge this or not. We need to be able to understand and accept them because they affect how we feel about ourselves and our fortunes, how we handle our new partnerships, as well as influencing our children's easy passage between their two parents. Time will be a great leveller, and you'll need to give yourself a considerable period before you can expect to feel fully adjusted to it all. This applies however ready you think you were for separating, though the feelings and attitudes that you're adjusting to will be different for each of you.

Both of you will need to accept that you must mourn the loss of the relationship. Mourning is not a negative process, it is a necessary pathway to feeling healed and resolved. You may cover up or deny feelings like sadness, anger and hurt because you think they're unmanly or weak or because you have the Anglo-Saxon 'stiff upper lip' way of masking emotions in the interests of controlled dignity. *If you do not allow yourself to experience the very real reactions to a major life event that draws on your coping resources very heavily, your adjustment, and therefore your future, will be affected in unhelpful ways.* If you cannot express feelings like grief, anger and sadness (all of which are normal reactions however much you wanted to separate), you may deny them by throwing yourself into work to an extent which cuts you off from human contact, and hence opportunities to resolve the feelings you're covering up. You may end up feeling isolated and depressed; angry and critical about your ex-partner, blaming their faults for your failure, unable to see the relationship any other way. Seeing yourself as a victim of your circumstances doesn't help you, and certainly won't help your children, and we saw in Chapter 5 how unresolved feelings can be unhelpfully transmitted to your children.

Mourning your lost relationship is like a sorting process. You have to note and acknowledge the positive and negative sides of a lost relationship in order to lay them aside and move on with your life positively. You must acknowledge the good bits of the relationship you now have to do without, even though you'd rather pretend you never valued these things instead of facing the discomfort of their loss. You may think that if you allow yourself to dwell on the positives, you'll start to feel anxious about your decision to leave, and you'd rather avoid more confusion and anxiety. Then you'll be likely to embellish your partner's faults to justify your position, and get stuck in a blaming frame of mind which inhibits your capacity to move forward.

Similarly, if you feel so overwhelmed with grief and self-blame about losing your partner, refusing to feel anger about it, you may cling to an idealised view of your life, only becoming happy again if your partner returns, and you'll feel bogged down by your sense of failure. This is obviously going to hold you up, inhibiting your relationships, affecting your parenting and work performance. For feelings to be laid aside they must first be identified, allowed and then they can be understood for what they mean. Otherwise they will remain in an unsorted jumble which continues to govern your life.

> I had what I thought was a really good relationship going with Peter, but we broke up six months ago. It was a friendly parting, but it took me a long time to recover. I found I was thinking about the relationship all the time and instead of it getting better as time went on. I was becoming more preoccupied, and my work performance went from bad to worse. We parted because I had told him how strong my feelings were for him and he felt we shouldn't go on seeing each other because he didn't feel as sure as I did about what we had together. I accepted this, but I kept on going over questions in my mind like whether if I hadn't told him how strong my feelings for him were, we might have been still together.
>
> He said he still wanted to be friends, but I said I didn't think we should have any contact while I sorted myself out. But I didn't seem to be able to sort anything out at all. I was afraid to make contact with him for fear he'd think I was chasing him. But I had to do something about not getting over him, it was ruining my life. Eventually I did contact him. I made sure I said that I wanted to ask him some questions for my own benefit, that I wasn't trying to persuade him to start again. The meeting went well and I clarified quite a few things. I felt much better afterwards. I still miss Peter and sometimes think I want him back, but I'm not nearly so preoccupied.

This story shows how you can get stuck if you don't have the opportunity to resolve a lost relationship. This woman had cut herself off from talking with Peter for fear of her difficult feelings. But this meant she couldn't come to understand what she'd done in the relationship, and her sadness and confusion stayed with her. Only once she was brave enough to address her questions within the relationship was it possible for her to move towards accepting her feelings about it and finish mourning its loss effectively.

The most effective way to handle any disappointment is to try and convince yourself that it has the power not only to cause pain, but also to teach you something useful about yourself—your vulnerabilities and your strengths—which enriches you. Allowing yourself to mourn about a profoundly disrupting experience, to accept and permit your reactions during your period of readjustment will enable you to do this. Despite what you may be feeling now, you will be able to feel positive about your past so you can start feeling positive about the future. And if you've applied even some of what you've read so far, you'll have made a better decision about your relationship. This will help you get there sooner.

Your aim is to be able to look back on your lost relationship free from bitterness with a philosophical detachment that enables you to say that you learned some useful things from it; that if you went back over the events that led up to and through the separation period, you wouldn't have done things very differently and that you did your best to handle it sensibly. To know what happened and why with reasonable clarity and how it affected you both is necessary to your recovery.

Once you've put into practice your separation arrangements, you may find you still want to spend time together. For a while there's no reason why you shouldn't do this. See it as part of the ongoing process of disengaging from your relationship. You may find yourself agreeing to meet because you feel your partner wants to, and you owe it to them, although you don't feel the need to do this yourself. Ask yourself how your meetings leave you feeling, and don't go on doing it for too long if you think it isn't helping you separate. It may be serving to sustain the relationship unhelpfully. Try and discuss together where seeing each other is taking you.

Re-establishing your social life

Many separated people are unsure of what to do about friends. Looking back on your time together you may realise that marriage and family life have absorbed you to the point where you haven't spent as much time actively cultivating outside friendships as you once did. Your partner was, in happier times, also your best friend, after all. Some valued people may have dropped from your circle because they didn't get on with your partner, or your partner didn't get on with them. Some of your friends won't know how to handle the fact that you're now apart and will hold back from contacting you. They may be anxious about how they'll react to the emotional side of what you're going through because your separation confronts them with feelings about their own relationship that they don't want to face. They may want to avoid taking sides, or feel that if they establish a separate kind of contact with you from now on, this will somehow prevent them from having a relationship with your partner as well. If you've been the prime mover in deciding to separate you may worry about how friends will view what you've done, afraid they may be judgemental about it.

You need friends more than ever now, they're a useful source of support, so try and take charge yourself of reaching out for contact. Make it easy for them to know where they stand with you and what contact you'd like to have. A worthwhile friend is one who respects you and will want to offer you companionship even if they don't understand why you've had to separate.

You may find you're apprehensive about new liaisons and embarrassed about your friends' efforts to pair you off. You may feel very strange and uncomfortable going out in groups unattached. Do this when you feel reasonably ready to, but don't add to your other challenges by forcing yourself to socialise when you really don't feel up to it. Expect to feel uneasy to begin with, and have a go. The sooner you give yourself the opportunity to have rewarding social contact, the kind that helps you feel valued for yourself, the better.

Becoming co-parents

If you have children you'll have to go on communicating with your 'ex'. You'll need time to adjust to a new way of relating. Because of the children you can't opt out of communicating with your 'ex' because it's irritating—you have to keep going. In one sense this keeps the relationship itself going when you'd otherwise have fully parted. What you do have to talk about—the children—is so important that there's plenty of scope for ongoing irritations. The many potential frustrations of estranged parenting can hold you back from detaching from the past, locking you into blaming your partner and worrying about the children more than is necessary, as well as limiting your passage to a brighter future. Even though you're both trying not to let what's left of your old feelings for one another interfere with your parenting responsibilities, when communication isn't all that good between you, you're going to get exasperated at times. This may be because you haven't been separated for all that long and you're both still feeling mistrustful. Or later on some old wounds may open up, interfering with communication. This sometimes happens when a major family event takes place like a remarriage or a house-move. You'll need some extra insight, patience and sensitivity. *Don't give up on trying to communicate with each other about the children.* Being able to talk without 'hanging up' is crucial, and it will get better, especially if you're willing to compromise a bit.

> We'd been separated for about eighteen months, and I'd been seeing the boys regularly at weekends. This had been going along quite well although I missed them dreadfully between visits. I thought of myself as having got over the break up fairly well and I was beginning to do new things with my life. But out of the blue I had a really unexpected reaction to something she did which affected my contact with the boys. She had a new man in her life, and they decided to move a two-hour drive away, and the travel time was going to cut into my time with them. It seemed reasonable to me that they should start coming on Friday nights so we didn't lose out on our time too much. I even offered to collect them, but Sue insisted this wasn't on because they'd be too tired after their school week, there'd be homework to fit in and they'd have a late night. I was hopping mad and all my old frustrations about her came flooding back. It just seemed so unfair that when it was her decision to move, we'd be the losers. I promised to get them home on time on Sundays, and to see that homework got done if she made sure they brought their books, but she wouldn't agree to it. I felt so powerless to do anything about her attitude, as if I was having to beg for time with my own children! It was one of the hardest things to cope with, calming down and realising that if I showed my anger and indignation it wasn't going to affect her reasoning about the situation. I had to accept what she said and just hope that once the new travelling routine was established, she'd reconsider.

You might be surprised at how, just when you thought you 'had it all together' about the past, irritations can resurface. The reappearance of 'divorce ghosts' is just a reminder of the reasons why you couldn't live together which crops up from time to time. Take a deep breath, remind yourself that you don't *have* to let your 'ex' get to you, and check with yourself whether whatever it is *really matters*! Put aside your exasperation about your partner, realise the fruitlessness of wanting things to be fair, of blaming yourself, your 'ex' or anybody else, and tackle life positively and with good humour for the children's benefit, as well as for the sake of your own dignity. Remember, for them to have a comfortable time despite the separation they don't need your disapproving views about their other parent coming through. Your partner's affairs and how they're conducting their life are nothing to do with you any more. The minute you hear something through the children or on the social grapevine, and you react with a judgement about it, stop and check whether you'd have had a quite different sort of reaction if it was someone else you'd heard was doing this. If the answer is yes, acknowledge that this is so, and note that you aren't as separated as you might think. Have another look at some of the ways your feelings can interfere with your parenting attitudes that were discussed in Chapter 5.

If you're seeing less of the children than you used to or would like to since you've separated, you'll face some especially hard adjustments. You may feel ill at ease and awkward with them to begin with, which is an uncomfortable reality. Time will help you feel more relaxed and enterprising with them if your discomfort is because you haven't ever been with them on your own much before. Try to think of this new kind of parenting as a challenge. The children need you to be positive, and this will also help you because it'll make your time together more rewarding. Avoid leaving too much of the caretaking to your new partner. It's you they need to be mostly with when they visit, especially to begin with.

Don't worry about Mum's new partner taking over your role as a father. It may hurt you terribly that he sees more of your children than you do, or that they call him Dad. Naturally this brings fears of being replaced, because there is the potential for a close relationship developing based on daily contact with a male adult who is close to Mum. But this relationship will not be a rival one unless the adults are in conflict about it. You are unlikely to be replaced in their hearts as father, unless you withdraw from your own commitment to the children. Try to be thankful that he's making the children's mother happy and that her happiness is good for them. See this person as an addition to your children's lives rather than a complication. If you can give your children joyful and positive experiences regularly—and try to see this time as separate and special for you all—there's no reason to think that the children will necessarily be confused or divided by having 'two fathers', especially if all of you are communicating about the children amicably when it's necessary to.

Keeping going

In the still of the night you'll probably sometimes feel it's all an incredible effort, and a tie which uncomfortably governs your social and working life. You'll ask yourself whether it's really all worth it. This part-time parenting seems like all give, and you don't seem to get much closeness back. Your children may sometimes feel like strangers, making it difficult to feel involved and in touch because you don't know anything about most of their lives. Perhaps you fear they only come and see you out of a sense of duty and not out of a real sense of belonging to you; you can't identify readily with some of the characteristics you see emerging in them as they grow older which you haven't yourself contributed to and would like to have 'counter-influenced'. You feel like only a half-parent.

Take heart. Children looking back on the experience of their parents' divorce often say that the one thing that made the whole business easier to bear was being able to freely go on seeing the parent they didn't live with most of the time. They need you. *If your relationship with your former partner is able to be cooperative for the sake of the lives you produced together, then in the long run it'll be well worth the effort it sometimes seems.* And it'll be fun. Children can develop strong bonds with a parent they don't spend all that much time with, especially if that time is spent well, and even if they have several other parent figures in their lives. Blood ties are strong, and although you may sometimes feel concerned at the apparent importance of a stepfather (or a stepmother) in your child's life, provided you are 'doing your bit', your child will never lose sight of the significance and value of a 'real' parent. *You are really contributing to your children's adjustment to their ongoing disappointment that you didn't stay together, as well as providing them with enriching experiences and perspectives they wouldn't otherwise have had.* And of course ensuring that they don't grow up thinking that they have a parent who isn't interested in them, or feeling a sense of worthlessness because they lost a valued relationship.

If you're the one who's doing more of the day-to-day caretaking (probably Mum), you'll have your own challenges to face with parenting on your own while sustaining the children's links with their father. Even if you did most of the parenting before you separated, continuing on your own still takes adjusting to. Sometimes you'll feel it's hard making all the day-to-day decisions alone, working constantly to run a home for several people, missing out on adult companionship, earning an inadequate income, sensitively managing all the children's daily ups and downs consistently and with the necessary authority, whilst combating inevitable fatigue. You'll sometimes feel it's a grind timetabling their contact with Dad, and perhaps resent them coming home excitable on Sundays full of stories of treats you'd never be able to afford. He seems to have all the freedom and all the pleasure-time with the children. Expect to feel this, and try to accept your feelings as part of the necessary adjustments of your new life.

Knowing when you've recovered

Here's a list of points, a 'resolution check list', to go through and see if you really are feeling okay about it all, and how far you've got with resolving issues left over from your relationship:

- I can think about my partner and appreciate the good things as well as the bad about our former relationship, without dwelling on them excessively.
- When I think about the reasons we couldn't stay together, I can see them as things I couldn't handle because of the way I am, rather than as unreasonable character defects in my partner.
- We can discuss necessary issues to do with the children without getting too exasperated. I don't find myself wanting to say how

my partner should be handling the children, but we can exchange useful information about them.

- I'm interested in what the children tell me about their time with my 'ex' because I want to share their joys and sympathise with their frustrations, not because I'm keen to learn about what's going on 'over there' out of my own curiosity.
- I can accept it when they don't say much. I'm not alarmist about things they might seem to be complaining about. I can see their remarks as having a variety of possible interpretations. I don't assume they necessarily reflect anything negative about their time with my 'ex'.
- I can encourage the children to enjoy their time with my ex-partner just as I would if they were going to spend time with a friend.
- I don't spend an excessive amount of time thinking about what my partner is doing with their life.
- I can accept the idea or the reality of their being with someone else.
- I don't look back on the arrangements we made for the separation, money and things, with any major regrets. Or if I do, I can accept that they seemed right at the time and it may not be worth going back and trying to re-arrange things.
- I am not constantly looking back and thinking things would be better if I'd handled them differently. I can accept that breaking up was difficult, and that there's often no ideal way to separate.
- I'm not unduly cautious or negative about new relationships, neither do I see getting into one as the cure-all to make me happy, to prove (especially to my 'ex') that I'm desirable.
- I don't feel any great need to talk about my separation, though I'm happy to answer people's questions.
- I feel my normal self when I'm talking to my 'ex'. I wouldn't cross the street to avoid contact, or seek out an excuse to contact them about something I could really handle myself.
- I think I can see my new partner in a realistic light without this spoiling the relationship, or I'm trying to do this.

If you can say yes or almost yes to most of these, you're well on the way to being detached, unembittered and positive about your life. Congratulations!

Starting over

If you haven't already, sooner rather than later most likely, you will fall in love again. We've seen how the involvement of someone else can affect both partner's reactions to separating in specific ways. A new partner often gets blamed for the original partnership breaking down, even if as far as you're concerned, the new friendship didn't get started till after you separated. You may not be able to change this view so don't waste too much time trying to. We've also seen how you can benefit by being separated for a while before you get seriously involved again. But of course new relationships do get going, often when you least expect it.

You may find that having spent quite some time preparing to make the right decision about your former relationship, you find it just as hard deciding to make a commitment to a new one. You've learned how disappointing and hurtful relationships can be! The way to approach this new kind of decision is the same: think, enquire, find out some facts, anticipate likely consequences, think again and go into it from an informed position with courage and optimism (and humour!). And as we've pointed out, a lot of what you thought about for separating can teach you useful things for deciding to make another commitment. Don't be put off by being uncertain. Anything worthwhile involves an element of risk. You cannot predict with complete certainty whether a relationship will work. You have to find out by trying. Allow some time to explore it further before you make a firm commitment. If your partner won't wait, and you want to be surer, ask yourself whether this pressure is fair, and whether you want a partner who can't accommodate your reasonable wishes. Look at the characteristics of relationships with good prospects in Chapter 4 and see how many of these you think you have or could find together.

Partners with pasts

You'll be curious about your new partner's 'ex', if they have one. Acknowledge a certain amount of curiosity as normal, and try to be open about talking about your respective pasts. However ideal the timing is, hopefully you'll be able to bring something useful into your new relationship from having been in a long-term relationship before, and see the merits of actively doing things for it to ensure its prospects of lasting.

It's more than likely that your new relationship will be even harder to get right, despite your experience and maturity, because it's very likely to be a package deal. You may have children who live with you most of the time, or your children may visit you regularly to be with you, and perhaps your new partner's children. Or your new partner may have children and you have no experience of them yourself. Both you and your 'ex' may have new partners each with their own children. It can be very complicated! The strange fact is that although stepfamilies are everywhere in increasing numbers, most people don't think about the possible complications of all these relationships before they commit themselves to taking them on. And many people say further down the track that they wish they had thought about the issues squarely much earlier so they could prepare for them. Partnerships are hard enough to get right, but in the optimistic glow of a new start, the extra complications of taking other people's feelings and attitudes into account, as well as those of your new partner, get forgotten. It's as if the mere existence of the new relationship will make everything about your extended family just take care of itself. You'll have extra high hopes after a failure, but more challenges to overcome.

Step relations

If you're contemplating making a commitment to a new relationship, *the first thing* you must do is accept that one or both of you have a past that can't be eradicated. Existing children are the source of powerful ties, strong feelings of frustration as well as joy, and are going to present considerable ongoing challenges to the new relationship. These challenges may end up damaging it if you're not careful. Don't make the mistake of not acknowledging this frankly. This relationship is not going to enjoy uninterrupted time for getting to know and trust each other before the arrival of children. Don't assume you will like your partner's children because you're in love with their parent, or that they'll automatically like you because you're making one of their parents happy.

Relationships don't just happen, they have to grow. Children don't have any choice about who their parents keep company with. However nice a step-parent they've acquired, their ongoing sadness that their biological parents didn't stay together means they need time to get used to new people in their lives, people who represent the permanence of their parents' separation. They are therefore going to elicit feelings and reactions in both parents and their new partners as they adjust to the new circumstances. This may catch you unawares and place unexpected pressure on your new relationship, not to mention on the children themselves and their transition between their two families.

> When I first moved in with James I was really enthusiastic about getting to know his children better, and having them come at weekends and be a sort of family together. I felt I could really help John with them, by being around doing all the motherly sorts of things like preparing nice meals and looking after their belongings. I wanted so much to please James and show him that I really accepted his past. I wanted to love his children, and didn't have any hang-ups about his ex-wife. But I think I tried too hard to be the perfect part-time Mum, and exhausted myself being well-prepared and available. Half the time my efforts weren't even noticed and I started to resent their regular intrusion into our normally peaceful lives, especially as we both work full-time. All I really wanted was to be with James at weekends on our own. And I found it difficult to know how strict to be with them, afraid that they'd resent me if I disciplined them.
>
> It's hard to be plunged into instant parenting with children you don't know very well, and I found it difficult to talk to James about my reactions to it all because I didn't want to undermine his relationship with the children by not being wholeheartedly positive about it. So tensions built up which started to affect our relationship, until I eventually did find the courage to discuss it with him.

Your *second step* is to find out how *you* really feel about your current parenting commitments, the good bits and the not-so-good. You'll have to work out how your new relationship will fit with these commitments, who you envisage will be responsible for what in the new family, how you expect your new partner to be with the children. Think about how you expect your new partner's relationship with your 'ex' to be now there are two same-sex parent figures, both involved in different ways with the children. Your children may soon have four parent figures in their lives, which can be enriching or debilitating for them and for the adult partnerships, depending on how you handle it from the beginning. Your partner may feel uncertain how to be, or how you want them to be, in relation to the children. You may be unsure of how much involvement your 'ex' will accept them having in relation to your children, or you yourself may be in that uncertain position. Think about all these important issues and decide what line you want to take with all of them. Get yourself a helpful handbook on step-parenting and blended families and find out more (and there's lots more) about what you're getting into.

Step three is to share all this with your new partner as openly and frankly as you can. Some people suppress any doubts or negative feelings they may have about other people's children, because they are ashamed of them or feel they may threaten the relationship, like James's new wife above. Expressing and acknowledging these as real, and not necessarily any reflection on the new partnership is very important and will help enormously further down the track.

Step four is to take things slowly. Everyone will take time to get used to new relationships, especially the children who are having to accommodate to having loyalties and affections in two places. When you want to move in together or get married, give the children some notice, listen to their feelings and accept their responses even if they're disappointing, and communicate your hopes for how it'll all work out. Let them get to know the new person at their own pace and don't spring a living together arrangement on them suddenly.

Step five is to make a commitment to continue looking after this relationship. You'll be doing this anyway now you've learned the hard way what can happen if you don't. This time the point is made to emphasise the importance of your solidarity as a couple at the head of a blended family, because the extra challenges of managing children, stepchildren and mixtures of both will test you to the limits sometimes. So it's extra important to regularly 'check-in' together on the problems and frustrations that are inevitable, so you can plan new strategies cooperatively and revise your existing policies.

Reflections

Having read this far, you may find yourself readier to make a wise decision, better equipped to make the many adjustments you face. You may react to what you've read by feeling overwhelmed with information and recommendations, but still unsure which way to go or how to cope. Perhaps you've said to yourself, 'Okay, it's all very fine in theory to say I should be doing this or that about relationships and feelings, but how do I actually go about being different or changing anything? I still feel stuck!'

Nothing about your life can be changed until you've acquired some new insight and understanding about the extremely complicated business of relationships and families. People don't acquire insight unless they're motivated to by a problem they face. Facing a critical turning point in your relationship is what prompted you to find out why you feel stuck and try to do something about it by thinking, asking questions, finding out more, and thinking again. *Anybody who's willing to reflect on their circumstances in ways which acknowledge other people's contribution as well as their own is doing something towards taking charge of their life.* They are emerging from the static position of avoiding their responsibility for themselves, passively blaming events and circumstances for their sense of frustration or lack of direction. Understanding the way things are and how much you contribute to them enables you to become more accepting of people and facts, and to make the changes of your choice.

Life involves many things we'd rather were different because they're hurtful, frustrating or limiting. Many of them can't be changed and certainly the past can't be undone. *You cannot go back and re-run your relationship better, but you can go forward in new ways.* Once you have some understanding and acceptance of the feelings and attitudes that made you react in self-limiting ways you'll be able to selectively modify those that aren't helpful to you or your partnerships. You'll begin to feel more detached and liberated. With this comes a powerful sense of being more in charge of yourself and your life, and more able to look forward and progress. You'll be more able to anticipate events and plan your life, rather than just reactively managing things as they arise. You'll be well on your way to being able to look back on difficult and painful times you've had, and see them as extensions and enrichments in your life rather than as traumas you'd rather lock away and forget.

However many new perspectives you've discovered, you probably won't be able to make the changes you want immediately. Almost everyone finds real and lasting changes hard to make. You need to reflect, discuss and consider yourself and relationships many times. You'll need time to absorb new insights, share them with your partner and friends, rehearse with yourself the resolutions you make, and you'll need practice. When you try out new ways of relating you probably won't manage everything you aimed for first time. Don't be discouraged if you feel tentative, or anxious that the different 'you' doesn't feel authentic or isn't always able to be consistent. Go over your attempt and work out why you didn't quite make it, and you'll get further next time. You're aiming to blend your new-found self-knowledge with having the courage of your convictions. Seeing the humorous side and being able to laugh at yourself will help you keep going.

Don't give up because there doesn't seem to be a right answer, a definite solution. Relationships are full of uncertainties, ambiguities, and mixed feelings and the issues they generate seldom have ready answers. When you've searched and thought and searched again, trying to make sense of what's going on and to anticipate the likely results of whatever options you think you have, *in the end what you must do is whatever makes you feel you're doing all you possibly can for yourself and your relationships in complex circumstances, without compromising beliefs and values that are important to you.*

You can't do much to change the way your partner is. Wishing they were different, and believing that if they were you'd have a better relationship isn't going to take the relationship very far that's useful. They can only change when they're ready to, not because you're asking them to. When you don't like the way your partner is handling things, whether it's how they approach attempts to discuss the relationship together or the way they're responding to the separation, remember that they are coping in their own way—just as you are—with the demands and challenges of relationships as they see them. The way they see them is part of why you may not be able to address things effectively and cannot stay together. Don't waste too much time battling against something you have no real power to change.

It's a mistake to neglect yourself in your efforts to be a successful partner, someone you think your partner will want to stay with. Looking after your own interests and working out what you want as well as what you can give isn't self-indulgent, it's constructive. Putting other people first all the time, something that committed partners often do believing that it will keep their partners happy, can make you feel frustrated, unappreciated or unfulfilled. You may not show this obviously or may not think you do, perhaps suppressing these feelings because you don't understand what they mean or think they're unworthy. Putting your partner and the family's needs first all the time may in fact make you just the sort of person your partner *doesn't* want.

You've put aside your own needs and selfhood in the service of the relationship, and all too often this paradoxically is what destroys it. And it certainly makes you vulnerable to being hurt for longer by a partner's rejection of you because you will feel it as a failing on your part. Counting on a relationship for all that you think you need to be a happy and satisfied person is asking more of a relationship than it can provide on its own. This is a pressure which may damage it beyond repair and leave you floundering for a long time because you've lost all you relied on in life.

Make sure you put yourself first sometimes, exploring and developing the individual creativity and potential that is uniquely yours and which gives you the ability to generate satisfaction and security from within yourself. This way you will be able to give a vitality and interest to a relationship that is uniquely individual, making you a more stimulating partner to be with because you have personal security of your own; someone who is more able to give enriching things to relationships for a long period of time; who is able to grow and develop with the rewards of a relationship, while their partner does the same.

Suggested reading

Abulafia, John, *Men and Divorce: Coping, learning and starting afresh*, Fontana Books, London, 1990

Burrett, Jill, *To and Fro Children: A guide to successful parenting after divorce*, Allen & Unwin, Sydney, 1991

Clarke, Michael, *Sexual joy: An intimate guide for couples*, Pan Books, Sydney, 1989

Heiman, Julia, and LoPiccolo, Joseph, *Becoming orgasmic: A sexual growth program for women*, Prentice Hall, New Jersey, 1988

Hendrix, Harville, *Getting the love you want: A guide for couples*, Schwartz and Wilkinson, Melbourne, 1988

Kingma, Daphne Rose, *Coming apart: Why relationships end and how to live through the ending of yours*, Conari Press, California, 1987

Kramer, Jonathan, and Dunaway, Diane, *Why men don't get enough sex and women don't get enough love*, Virgin Books, London, 1991

Lerner, Harriet Goldhor, *The dance of intimacy: A woman's guide to courageous acts of change in key relationships*, Harper and Row, New York, 1989

Litvinoff, Sarah, *The Relate guide to better relationships*, Ebury Press, London, 1991

Montgomery, Bob, and Evans, Lynette, *Living and loving together*, Penguin Books/Viking O'Neil, Australia, 1989

Montgomery, Bob, and Morris, Laurel, *You and sex*, Penguin Books/Viking O'Neil, Australia, 1991

Norwood, Robin, *Women who love too much*, Arrow Books, London, 1986

Peck, M. Scott, *The road less travelled*, Arrow Books, London, 1990

Stafford, David, and Hodgkinson, Liz, *Codependency: How to break free and live your own life*, Piatkus Books, London, 1991

Tannen, Deborah, *You just don't understand: Women and men in conversation*, Virago Press Ltd, London, 1990

Webber, Ruth, *Living in a stepfamily: Stepparents' handbook*, Australian Council for Educational Research Ltd, 1989